THE WORLD, THE FLESH, AND FR. SMITH

BRUCE MARSHALL

THE WORLD,
THE FLESH,
AND
FR. SMITH

SOPHIA INSTITUTE PRESS
Manchester, New Hampshire

Cover Designer: Updatefordesign Studio

Cover art: *Illustration of People in the Rain* by Nadezda Grapes (Depositphotos 201441808); Christianity Set by Paula13 (Depositphotos 23626363)

Sophia Institute Press
Box 5284, Manchester, NH 03108
1-800-888-9344
www.SophiaInstitute.com

Sophia Institute Press is a registered trademark of Sophia Institute.

paperback ISBN 978-1-64413-836-6

ebook ISBN 978-1-64413-837-3

Library of Congress Control Number: 2023933270

For Sheila,
Who may one day
read this book

Contents

THE WORLD, THE FLESH, AND FR. SMITH

I

AS HE FREEWHEELED down the long hill, Father Smith remembered with irritation that, as a member of the League of Saint Columba, he had promised to say a *Pater*, an *Ave*, and a *Gloria* daily for the conversion of Scotland. There was no dispensation either on Sundays, not even for priests who had to bicycle twenty miles on an empty stomach to say two Masses and preach two sermons in separated parishes, who had their Office to recite as well, and another sermon and benediction to give in the evening. "Our Father, Who art in Heaven," he began, but he gave it up before he had proceeded more than one or two clauses, because the rain was dripping down the back of his neck and because he felt that praying for the conversion of Scotland never seemed to do much good anyway, as, for all the intercession of the Blessed Virgin, Caledonia, stern and wild, continued, in 1908, to remain as unimaginatively Presbyterian and unsanctified as before. What could even God and all His saints make of a country that preferred the metrical version of the Psalms to inspired English or Latin and whisky to wine? Was it not Hilaire Belloc who had written:

> Where'er a Catholic sun doth shine
> There's always laughter and good red wine,

At least I have always found it so,
Benedicamus Domino.

He would like to quote the version in a sermon, but supposed that
if he did, he would probably be misunderstood, especially by those
who had responded to Monsignor O'Duffy's: "My dear brethren
in Jesus Christ, it begins with a thimbleful and it ends with a
bucketful, as all good Kartholic drunks have had to avow in the
Holy Sarkrament of Penance."

Instead, he began to pray for the souls of all those who must
die and be judged that day, one hundred and forty thousand of
them, according to the statistics. This he never found difficult,
because he was filled with pity for so many ignorant blasphemers,
liars, cowards, misers, successful business men, and fornicators
who must wake up, in the last flutter of an eyelid, to the awful
realization that Revelation was really true, after all, and that the
graph of their compromisings, bibblings, cruelties, wenchings,
and tattlings was going to be read out to them by Almighty God
Himself. "Je vous offre toutes les messes qui se célèbrent
aujourd'hui dans le monde entier pour les pauvres pécheurs qui
sont maintenant à l'agonie et qui doivent mourir ce même jour,"
he murmured, using, as always, the French prayer he had once
seen hanging up on the porch of a Breton church, and thinking of
all the forgetful people he saw daily walking with vacant eyes along
the ugly streets. For it was people like that who were dying: dull
men in Moscow and Madrid, raddled old women in Perth and
New York, gathered into God's basket like so many surprised,
gasping fish. Of course, they wouldn't all go to Hell any more than
they would all go to Heaven. There was Purgatory, wherein the
weak and the worldly were made clean, because even the best of
men couldn't hope to go clod-hopping straight into God's

presence after spending a lifetime talking about umbrellas and colds in the head.

"Que le sang précieux de Jésus Rédempteur leur obtienne miséricorde et pardon." But, in spite of the Precious Blood of Jesus, some people, the willfully bowler-hatted and the blind, the oppressors of the poor, politicians and bank presidents, lechers and lewd women on high sofas, seemed bound to go plumb down to Hell, because they had died in the state of final impenitence, which was the sin against the Holy Ghost. And Hell, according to the theologians, was a very unpleasant place indeed. Sorer than the sorest pain that had ever been suffered in the world and going on forever and ever. "Imagine being simultaneously burned alive and having your nails torn out and your entrails wound through a pronged mangle and having your eyes gouged out and your limbs pulled apart by horses and knowing that the pain would never stop—well, no Gaiety girl's worth that, is she?" Monsignor O'Duffy had once told the men's guild in Tobermory. The bishop, however, had been inclined to take a more tolerant view. "All we really know about Hell is that it is a state that exists," he had once told Father Smith when they had been climbing Ben Nevis together. "We know that Hell exists because God has told us so, and God can neither deceive nor be deceived. But we are not bound to believe that there is anybody in it. Even to Judas Iscariot, God may have granted the grace of final repentance between his falling from the tree and his bowels gushing out. And even if there are poor, unfortunate souls in Hell, we are, I think, entitled to believe that their agonies are spiritual rather than physical. For the essence of Hell is separation from God, and even unbelievers and sinners shall love God in Hell and feel their loss of Him. Indeed, a Spanish priest once told me that he thought it not unlikely that the damned would be punished in Hell by being forced to practice for all eternity those very vices through whose indulgence on earth they had forfeited Heaven. And sometimes, Father, when out of Christian charity and social politeness I have to listen to the conversation of worldlings, I am not sure that he wasn't right. From an unsupernatural standpoint, the chief grumble I've got against sin is that it's so boring."

The approach to the town lay through rows of long, damp, depressed streets, each so dismal that Father Smith found it both easy and difficult to understand why their inhabitants did not try to lead Christian lives: easy, because there was nothing about those streets to inspire men to the pursuit of the good and the beautiful; difficult, because the lack of inspiration should have been itself an inspiration, since it ought to have occurred to the beholders of such ugliness that life could not possibly have been intended to be so meaningless. Although the church bells were already ringing, there were few worshippers abroad in these streets, because the Church of Scotland had long ago lost the allegiance of the industrial poor. Here and there a few newsagents' shops were open, with pyramids of Gold Flake boxes and walking-sticks in the window. In the doorway of a tenement, a brilliantined young Jew stood swinging a yellow cane. Father Smith said a prayer for him, too, as he passed, although he didn't think it would do much good.

Down along the tramlines he sped, down past the hoardings shouting Wincarnis and Van Houten, down, down, down, with here and there another Father Smith sailing briefly through the blue or the green glassy sea of an ironmonger's or a fruiterer's blinded window. In the center of the town, the burgesses were out in their morning coats and top hats and their wives with their feather boas and their bored young sons and their prunes-and-prisms young daughters, all trooping staunchly along under the bells to worship the God of Bethel and Balmoral and porridge and bagpipes and kilts and preference shares in jute companies. Father Smith prayed for them, too, as he passed, because he knew that they weren't really bad but only slothful and selfish and stupid, and that there had once been something rather fine and noble about Calvinism, when men had erred in doctrine through a desire to speak with God. Past the gaunt High Kirk he sped, with the elders standing beside the collection plates at the open door, past the Episcopal Church of the Holy Trinity, where all the real nobs went, on until he come to more newsagents and the slums and the docks, on until he came to the fruit market that had been hired out by the town council to the Catholics on Sundays so that the holy sacrifice of the Mass might be offered and Christ come again through the morning in the swift white sacrament of His love.

The outside of the fruit market was often covered with bawdy monosyllables, but Father Smith had never paid much attention to them because he knew that they hadn't been intended as an insult to God. Today, however, he noticed that there were anti-religious challenges as well, such as: "To Hell with the Pope," and one whose misspelling made him smile: "No Popery aloud." He knew that there had been opposition on the part of certain influential bigots to the letting-out of the fruit market to the Catholics, but he didn't suppose that anyone very important had scrawled those crude letters. The sacristan, however, who was laying out the vestments in the shut-off space behind the packing cases, took a grave view of the matter.

"There's trouble in the air, Father," he said, as the priest took from his bag the little cruet containing the unswallowed ablutions from his first Mass at Drumfillans. The sacristan was a knobbly old sailor who had led the life of a saint all over the seven seas and the world's most stinking ports. "Airchie Tamson and yon crowd of his are out for trouble."

"Well, well, if trouble comes, it'll keep our religion from getting rusty," Father Smith said. "That's the great thing about persecution: it keeps you up to the mark. It's habit, not hatred, that is the real enemy of the Church of God."

"All the same, I'd like fine to get the same Airchie Tamson a guid bang on the heid," the sacristan said.

Father Smith did not answer but bundled into his alb, flung a violet stole over his shoulders, and went down to the other end of the market to hear confessions because, although it was a sung Mass, Holy Communion was to be given, as there had been no other Mass earlier in the day. As he sat on his lonely chair, shriving old women whose thoughts had wandered during their prayers and young men who had slipped their hands inside girls' bodices, the priest could hear Miss O'Hara testing out the cock-and-hen choir on the *Agnus Dei*. "Tum-tum, now all together: 'Angus Dei, Qui tollis peccata mundi.'" The singing, as usual, was almost as bad as the accents, but Father Smith was sure that Almighty God would hear it with a lenient ear, because every false note was meant as praise, which was not always true of trillings from hired sopranos in Milan, Seville, and Vienna.

"Father, I'm downright ashamed of myself and I'm sorry, but I know fine I'll do it again," an unhappy male voice came through the wire netting that the postman had detached from a rabbit hutch and nailed over the hole on the old pierrot ticket office to do duty for a grill.

"My child, of course you know that you'll do it again, because you're relying on yourself and not on God's grace," the priest said. "Pray for God's grace, pray to Our Lady, come frequently to Holy Communion, and you'll be surprised at the progress you'll make."

"I'll do my best, Father, but if God kens as much about me as I ken about myself, He must ken fine I'm damned already," the voice said. "And in any case, He must ken already because He's God and kens everything before it happens like."

"That, of course, is true," Father Smith said. "Almighty God knows already whether each one of us is saved or damned, since omniscience is an attribute of His omnipotence; but that does not alter the fact that each one of us will be saved or damned of his own free will, although God knows beforehand how we shall use our free will. It's like a man standing on a railway bridge watching an express train coming down the line and a cow crossing a field toward the line. The man knows that the cow will be killed, but the cow has still the free will to turn aside and not be killed, although the man also knows that the cow is too stupid to use her free will and turn aside and not be killed. For your penance, you will say one Our Father and three Hail Marys. And now make your act of contrition while I give you absolution."

"Thanks, Father. And I'll try not to forget yon bit about the cow."

Miss O'Hara was still drilling her choir when Father Smith left the confessional, but she stopped as soon as she saw the priest approaching.

"I think I've got them all right now, Father, although the introit is still a little creaky," she said.

"I'm sure they'll be excellent," the priest said, and he smiled at Miss O'Hara and at the whole tired, earnest choir with their squee-gee hats and pouter-pigeon throats. The choir smiled back, because they liked the priest and thought that it was grand fun being able to praise the Lord in loud, rumbling Latin.

The priest thought of the penitents whom he had just shriven as he walked away back down through the congregation to vest for Mass, and he prayed for them that they might be given strength to go on struggling against their sins. Back in his makeshift sacristy, however, he thought of the great sacrifice of God's Body and

Blood that he was going to offer and of the sweet, ineffable, unfailing mystery that his own unworthy, human, consecrated hands were about to perform.

The scrabble of acolytes were already in their scarlet cassocks and white cottas and were jostling and tumbling, although they were quite pious boys really and never passed the Blessed Sacrament without genuflecting and took it in turn to serve Father Smith's weekday Mass, which was said in the schoolroom. Three of them were caddies on the golf course and one was a fishmonger's boy, and they generally went about together, since it was difficult going about with Protestant boys, as they had to try and love our Lord and not tell dirty stories because they were Catholics. Father Smith looked at them and loved them as he took off his violet stole and put on a green one, crossing it under his girdle to represent Christ's Passion and death. Then he put on a big, faded, green cope, which Monsignor O'Duffy had sent down to him from the pro-cathedral because a wealthy publican had presented the chapter with a shimmering new one, with alpha and omega embroidered in scarlet and gold on the hood.

The congregation stood up as Father Smith marched in to give the asperges, with Tim O'Hooley and Angus McNab holding back the sides of his cope. "Asperges me," he intoned in his throaty voice, which the bishop had once said he was afraid would never be quite the real Mackay, and Miss O'Hara and her billiard markers, insurance touts, and untouched virgins zoomed and screeched back: "Domine, hyssopo, et mundabor."

Down through the files of the faithful went Father Smith, with Patrick O'Shea walking in front, carrying the bucket of holy water. Railway porters, dockers, sailors, schoolmistresses, shopgirls, and servant girls all crossed themselves as the silver glistening blobs came flicking out at them. Across hats and shawls and bold bald pates the priest sprinkled the holy water, symbolically washing them from their weekday thoughts and ambitions, out across the old women at the back wearing their husbands' tweed caps stuck on with a big pin, because, although Saint Paul had said that a woman's crowning glory was her hair, he had also said that she ought to keep it covered when she went into the house of the Lord. To the three chorus girls with hair like wood shavings Father Smith gave a special sprinkle because he thought their pale, yellow faces looked so awful, and to Professor Brodie Ferguson in the third row because he thought that the metaphysician suffered from intellectual pride.

In the green chasuble with a lamb on the back, which from a distance looked like a horse, in the little house of charity, with his hands joined, Father Smith began the Mass, confessing to Almighty God, to blessed Mary ever virgin, to blessed Michael the Archangel, to blessed John the Baptist, to the holy apostles Peter and Paul, to Tim O'Hooley, Angus McNab, Patrick O'Shea, and the blistered old charwoman kneeling in the draught at the back, that he had sinned exceedingly in thought, word, and deed, through his fault, through his fault, through his own most grievous fault. The choir ironed out, flattened, tore asunder, and sent bellying up to Heaven like a shriek from a dying pig the introit for the third Sunday after Epiphany, "Adorate Deum, omnes angeli eius," right on to "Laetentur insulae multae," and then wheezed forth the *Kyrie* while Father Smith took the thurible from Angus McNab and blessed the incense and sent it whirling in fragrant blue puffs up to the throne of God.

It was raining again outside, and Father Smith could hear the heavy drops on the corrugated-iron roof as he crossed to sing the Gospel. When he turned to preach the sermon, he saw that some of the congregation were sitting with their umbrellas up because the roof was leaking in places. He read through the notices at a rate because he didn't want the faithful to get too wet, and he knew that few ever listened anyway. Then, when he had read the Epistle and Gospel in English, he began his sermon.

"All the glory of the king's daughter is in golden borders; clothed round about with varieties. In the Name of the Father, and of the Son, and of the Holy Ghost, Amen." Father Smith knew that at the best of times he was no preacher, and this morning, after having preached and said one Mass already and cycled twenty miles and all on an empty stomach, he despaired of his ability to ram home the reality of the beauty of the Church of God into the porridge of holy, thoughtless Italo-Irish poltroons that faced him. As he hesitated after giving out his text, a baby began to whimper at the back, and from the empty, godless street outside came the moan of an urchin singing that winter's pantomime success:

> "If I should plant a tiny seed of love
> In the garden of your heart ..."

"The universality of the Church of God is a fact for which Catholics ought never to cease to give thanks. It is perhaps hard for us in this rusty, ramshackle fruit market in sorry, separated Scotland to realize that in our worship, faith, and doctrine we are at one with the great congregations in the cathedrals of Europe. No bishop in Chartres, no cardinal in Burgos or Warsaw, nay, my dear brethren, no pontiff in Rome, no, not even the Holy Father himself, consecrates more surely bread to Christ's Body and wine to Christ's Blood than do I, your unworthy parish priest. It is a thought that ought to make us both proud and humble: proud because we alone among our fellow countrymen are in step with European tradition and speak the good, sane grammar of God; humble because we of ourselves have done nothing to deserve so glorious a privilege."

Looking out over the faces at which he was preaching, he saw that they were looking neither proud nor humble, although here and there a mouth gaped and an eye peered. The three chorus girls sat with their faces spooned up under their hats, and Professor Brodie Ferguson had his eyes screwed up and his nose wrinkled, probably because he thought he knew all about the Church of God already. Several women were openly reciting the Rosary, clicking their beads along on top of their muffs.

"Yet it is not the universality of the Church that makes its doctrine true. If only one person in the whole world accepted the teaching of the Church, that doctrine would still be true. If nobody at all believed the teaching of the Church, the mathematic of faith would still be as true as was the law of gravity before Newton discovered it. For faith is not a sort of competition in a magazine, to which the various sects send in their doctrinal guesses and hope for the best; it is belief in revelation on the authority of God Himself." The chorus girls' faces and the professor's nose were still unimpressed, and at the back of them all, the baby began to howl as though its mother were prodding it with pins.

Perhaps it was his rhetoric that was at fault, Father Smith thought as he meandered on. Or perhaps it was just that it was the hardest thing in the world for one human being to shine into another human being the glow that burned within himself, even when the glow was from God. Yet surely these Catholics to whom he was preaching and who had to suffer criticism and hatred in a land that spurned their faith, surely they must understand that in the spread of their religion lay the world's one sure hope, since the Church spoke the same things to all men in all tongues.

"So," he concluded, "so we may make for our own the words of the psalmist, when he sings of the future Bride of Christ in the words that I have chosen for my text today. 'All the glory of the king's daughter is in golden borders, and she is clothed round about with varieties.' But let us remember that the golden borders are there to honor Almighty God and not men. The priest wears rich vestments at Mass and incense is burned because Christ is coming on the altar and must be met with symbols of love and reverence, rickety and inadequate as they may be. And even if the symbols weren't there, even if a priest were to say Mass in rags and tatters, the king's daughter would still be in golden borders, because Christ would be there as He promised when He said: 'Lo, I am with you all days, even unto the consummation of the world.' Thus, in this our rented tabernacle, we know that God will come to His tryst; but we know also that it is our duty to provide a more fitting dwelling place for Him, and so we hope that it will soon be possible for us to build a church of our own where we may worship Him and adore. A blessing that I wish you all in the Name of the Father, and of the Son, and of the Holy Ghost, Amen."

The priest felt happier as he turned back to go on with the Mass and began the *Credo*, because now he knew that he was again on rails and could not fail. Yet was not the very certainty of the hard, fast, safe words that he was going to utter itself fraught with danger, since it was so easy to say them carelessly? As he sat on the sedilia with his hands palm-downward on his knees and his biretta big and black and bold on the back of his head, listening to Miss O'Hara's cocks and hens bawling "Genitum non factum," he remembered having read somewhere that the first time Robert Hugh Benson had sung High Mass in Westminster Cathedral, he had felt sure that he had committed a mortal sin, because he had been paying more attention to music than to meaning. "Et in vitam venturi saeculi, amen." With the tail of his chasuble flipping out behind him, Father Smith returned to the altar.

With his arms spread like Christ's upon the tree, he prayed for the living, for Professor Brodie Ferguson and Miss O'Hara and the three chorus girls and Mr. Balfour and Mr. H. G. Wells and old Mrs. Flanigan who kept the lodging-house on John Knox Street and hadn't been to Mass since she had had her ingrown toenail cut out, that they might be granted fellowship with John, Stephen, Matthias, Barnabas, Ignatius, Alexander, Marcellinus, Peter, Felicity, Perpetua, Agatha, Lucy, Cecily, and Anastasia. The mystery was quickly over. Saints' names came and went like windows lit with God, and God Himself in the orbit of His own chosen understandment. With his arms spread and his thumbs and forefingers joined, the priest prayed that the servants and handmaids of the Lord who had gone before in the sign of faith might rest in Christ and that to those whose souls and whose bodies had once itched and sinned far back beneath forgotten Spanish moons God might grant a place of refreshment, light, and peace. Then, when he had communicated himself, he was away from the altar and along the altar rails, popping the frail flake of Christ into the mouths of saints and sinners that Christ might keep their bodies and souls until life everlasting, because nothing else mattered.

He was happy when he was back in the sacristy and out of his vestments, because now the load of his priesting was lifted and he was able to say glad, lovely words in the thanksgiving: "Trium puerorum cantemus hymnum, quem cantabant sancti in camino ignis, benedicentes Dominum." But while he was calling upon the sun and the moon, shower and dew, fire and heat to bless the Lord, the sacristan came and told him that there were two babies waiting at the back to be baptized, so he had to scamper through the rest of his prayer, right down to "praise him on well-sounding cymbals," and hoped that God would pardon him for his haste, because God must know just as well as he did that it was important for babies to be baptized.

There was quite a clutter of hats and boas and new blue waistcoats and watchchains and creaky shoes round the portable font when Father Smith reached it in cotta and stole, and the babies themselves, with closed eyelids and spittle on their lips. One baby was a girl, the daughter of Paolo Sarno, the Italian ice-cream merchant, and the other was a boy, the son of James Scott, driver of the Corporation tramways. The two families readily agreed to Father Smith reading the main part of the service for both babies at once, but of course he said that he would put the salt on their tongues and baptize them separately, because that was the part that gave them a chance of becoming saints and living with God forever and ever in Heaven.

Before he began the service, he spoke a few words to the parents of the baby girl in Italian, because he had been trained at the Scots College in Rome and loved speaking the language. The women's dark eyes glowed, and the men smiled and showed their very white teeth, because they liked the idea of their baby being baptized by a priest who knew how to speak Italian. Father Smith spoke to the tramway driver and his men friends and womenfolk, too, and pressed the Scots baby's nose twice as many times as he had pressed the Italian baby's, in case they should be jealous at his having spoken so much to the other parents in a language that they didn't understand. Then he opened his *rituale* and hared off down the *Ordo Baptismi Parvulorum*, because he was hungry and in a hurry for his lunch, which he knew that he couldn't have until he had transformed the two children before him into potential saints and inheritors of the Kingdom of Heaven.

His thoughts wandered once or twice during his recitation of the rapid Latin, but they wandered in the right direction, and he knew that the Lord couldn't really be angry with him, because he was thinking about Baptism and not about his lunch. "Exorcizo te, creatura salis, in nomine Dei Patris omnipotentis . . ." How easy Baptism was, and how kind God had been to institute so simple a sacrament, and how heavy were the responsibilities of godparents and how lightly they took them as a general rule! But that was just Almighty God's way of doing things: He sent sanctifying grace down in great splashes so that the silver shining puddles lay about all over the earth for people to tramp through or stoop and drink as their dispositions gave them perception. What were these two babies he was baptizing now going to become? Were they going to be for Christ or against Him or followers of the middle way, bowing both to God and Mammon. "Accipe sal sapientiae." The baby girl whimpered as she tasted the salt, but the boy took it greedily, opening his bright blue eyes in mild surprise. The parents creaked in their new shoes and stared at the priest out of dull, vegetable eyes. Father Smith named the two infants in Christ for all eternity as he poured the water over their brows, baptizing Elvira Maria Francesca and Joseph Dominic Aloysius in the Name of the Father and of the Son and of the Holy Ghost. Once again the girl whimpered, but the boy was unperturbed. Father Smith had turned his stole from the violet side to the white side as a sign that Satan and all his works and pomps had been renounced. He finished the service, praying away happily. When he had finished, the Italians were all over him with "Grazie tante," but the tramway driver, James Scott, stood aside and remained behind even when the members of his family had left.

"Father, I'd like to show my gratitude to you," he said as he pressed a crisp note into the priest's hand. "I know you won't take it for yourself, but take it for that new church you're soon going to start building, please."

Father Smith never liked taking money from his parishioners, even for holy purposes, because he felt that praying and doing God's glad work was an easy way of earning one's living compared with scrubbing floors or driving tramway cars, but he took the money all the same, because he knew that the tramway driver would have been insulted if he hadn't and that God needed a fitting home anyway.

The sacristan was waiting for him with a worried look when he came back to unvest.

"Father, there's an old sailor dying at Mistress Flanigan's and the auld besom's sent a laddie for to tell ye to come at once."

With difficulty, Father Smith repressed a snort of impatience. He was hungry and he was tired and he had been long enough a priest to bear a grudge against sinners for always choosing to die at awkward moments—in the middle of the night or when a poached egg had just been served. He remembered, however, the shock with which he had once heard Father Bonnyboat say on an Easter Sunday, "I'm sick to death of giving Holy Communion," and reminded himself that death was no less death to the sinner who was dying because others had died before him, and that he was Christ's priest who had been marked and anointed and ordained to save human souls.

As he had no permanent church, Father Smith had to reserve the Blessed Sacrament in Montrose Street, where he had rented two rooms for a presbytery. Tearing out of his cassock, he hurried away on his bicycle. The streets were still slippery and slimy from the rain, and his back tire skidded twice, and once his front wheel got caught in the tram line. Even when she heard that someone was dying, his landlady wanted him to have his lunch first, saying that the roast beef would spoil if it were kept in the oven much longer, but the priest told her sharply that the fate of a human soul was much more important than any amount of roast beef, and he rushed into the chapel, where with blundering fingers he plucked a Host out of the ciborium and hung it in a silver pyx round his neck and under his coat. He also took the holy oils with him as well, to anoint the sailor's eyes, ears, nose, mouth, hands, and feet and cleanse him from his sins of sense.

Because it was raining again when he came out, he took the tram because there was a direct line to John Knox Street, and he didn't want to run the risk of a fall when he was carrying the Blessed Sacrament. The tram was empty because the Presbyterians and the Episcopalians had been out of church for a long time now, and it was still a bit early for the brilliantined young men and their girls. The conductor took the priest's fare sullenly and then stood at the back whistling through his teeth and reading *Photo-Bits*. The tram zoomed and lurched away down the street with Father Smith making acts of adoration to the Blessed Sacrament opposite a stained-glass advertisement for Odol.

The priest knew that Mrs. Flanigan's lodging-house on Knox Street was not all that it should be, but he had no hesitations about taking the Blessed Sacrament there, because real sinners always knew how to respect our Lord and because our Lord Himself had been in even lower dives when He had lived on earth. Mrs. Flanigan was at the door to receive him, in a fine state of sweat and nerves and holding a monster lighted candle in her hand, because she knew that the priest would be carrying the Host.

"Praise be to Jasus, you've come, Father," she said. "It was only this morning that I found out that he was a Catholic and I sent for your riverence as soon as the doctor told me he was dying. Faith and he's lying cursing and swearing fit to burst himself, he is and all, but I've no doubt that yon'll be pleased enough to see you when you tell him who you are."

The priest nodded and followed Mrs. Flanigan along the passage, which smelled of brussels sprouts and linoleum. From an open door, three pretty girls in dressing gowns poked tousled heads, and two of them curtsied and crossed themselves because, although they were bad girls, they didn't hate God at all and knew that it was Jesus of Nazareth Who had walked on the Sea of Galilee Who was passing by. "Faith, ye trollops, and let the holy praist bay, will ye now," Mrs. Flanigan shouted at them as she pulled the door shut, because she wanted Father Smith to imagine that it was a hotel she ran.

In the bedroom where the sailor lay dying, Mrs. Flanigan had already placed a crucifix, two lighted candles, and a glass of water on the bed-table, because she always kept these things handy, since she didn't want to run any risks when the Lord called upon her to kick the bucket herself. The sailor himself was a very ill sailor, and he lay on a high bed in a pair of widely striped pajamas. Lying there with his eyes closed, his face looked not unlike the face of His Holiness Pope Pius X, but Father Smith suspected that the thoughts that went on behind it were slightly different. When he had laid the pyx and the chrism on the linen cloth, the priest motioned to Mrs. Flanigan to leave him alone with the dying man. When she had gone, he sat down beside the bed and took the old sailor's hand in his. The sailor's hand was very hot, and Father Smith felt very sorry for him being so ill and dying, but he knew that there was no time to be lost.

"My child, I've come to hear your confession," he said.

The old sailor opened a pair of very blue eyes. They appeared to take some time to interpret the priest's presence, but when they succeeded, they grew dark and angry.

"Leave me alone, won't you," the old sailor said, half-raising himself from his bed and falling back again.

Father Smith smiled wearily. Fifteen years ago when he had been a young priest carrying the Blessed Sacrament to deathbeds, protests like this had both shocked and frightened him, because it had been hard for a young priest of twenty-five with strong black hair to reconcile hoary sinners with God. But the strong black hair was peppered with gray now, and he had knocked about with his Lord in all corners of the vineyard and had learned a thing or two about motives of pride and human respect.

"My son, you are dying, and nobody is going to think you a fine fellow any longer for denying our Blessed Lord," he said. "The time for acquiring merit is short. I am God's priest, and I am here to hear your confession."

As he had expected, his words had an almost immediate effect. The hostile glare vanished from the old sailor's eyes, and he turned his head away from the priest and said:

"It's true, Father. I've been all sorts of a dirty swine, but it's too late now."

"It's never too late as long as you're alive," Father Smith said. "That's just where God's mercy comes in." But did it? Mightn't it have been a bit more merciful on God's part to have set a time limit on repentance, say forty-five? There would have been no inducement for sinners to keep putting things off to the last moment then, and it would have been a lot easier for priests. Father Smith smiled briefly at his own impertinence and rather imagined that God was smiling too, and then he got back to the dreary business of getting a not very original sinner to acknowledge his sloth, his stupidity, and his cowardice.

It was obvious at once that the sailor had not been practicing his religion for years, because he said right away that he didn't remember when he had last been to Mass or Holy Communion, although he had never gone to sleep without saying a Hail Mary, because out East a fellow never knew when he wouldn't wake up with his throat slit. Then he started off to tell the priest about all the women he had known in Buenos Aires and Hong Kong and said that he had liked the women in Hong Kong best, but Father Smith said that he thought they had better go through the Commandments from the beginning and see how many he had broken because, after all, it was a bigger mortal sin to have forgotten to love God all one's life than to have known tawdry Jezebels in foreign ports. The sailor said that that was quite easy and that there was no need to go through the Commandments at all, because he had broken the whole lot of them right down to coveting his neighbor's ass, and that Father Smith was quite wrong, as the women weren't tawdry at all, especially the ones in China, who had had gold on their fingernails and worn black satin slippers with high red heels, and that now that he came to think of it, he wasn't sorry for having known all these women at all, since they had all been so beautiful and that he would like to know them again if he got the chance. Father Smith said that that was very wrong of the sailor and that our Lord and our Lady and Saint Joseph and the saints were very much more beautiful than any number of Chinese harlots with high heels; but the sailor said that he wasn't so sure, and that he still wasn't sorry for having known all these women, because their dresses had made such lovely sounds when they walked, and in South America, it had been much the same thing, and the governor general had seemed to think so too, because he had always been at old Señora Alvarez's every Saturday night. The priest said that was no way for a man to talk to God when he was dying and that the old sailor had better hurry up and be sorry for his sins if he didn't want to go to Hell and lose Almighty God forever and ever; but the old sailor said that while he was sorry for having missed the sacraments so often and for not having loved God more, he wasn't sorry for having known all those women, because they had all been so beautiful and some of them very kind as well. In despair, Father Smith asked the old sailor if he was sorry for not being sorry for having known all these women, and the old sailor said that yes he was sorry for not being sorry and hoped that God would understand. Whereupon Father Smith said that he thought that perhaps God would understand, and he absolved the old sailor from his sins, pouring the merits of Christ's Passion over the old sailor's forgetfulness of God and those long-ago dresses that had made such lovely sounds.

It was easy enough to anoint the old sailor, because he lay quite still and seemed to like it when Father Smith took the holy oil of chrism and healed his limbs and his senses from walking away from and touching away from and hearing and seeing and smelling away from Jesus for so long; but it wasn't so easy for the old sailor to swallow the Blessed Sacrament, because his mouth was dry and parched, and Father Smith had to help him by making him drink some water afterward. Then the old sailor seemed to sink into unconsciousness, although Father Smith knew that he was still alive because the stripes on his pajamas kept going up and down. Kneeling beside the bed, the priest began to recite the prayers for the dying: "Go, Christian soul, from this world, in the Name of God the Father Almighty, Who created thee; in the Name of Jesus Christ, the Son of the Living God, Who suffered for thee; in the Name of the Holy Ghost, Who was breathed into thee; in the name of the glorious and holy virgin Mother of God, Mary; in the name of blessed Joseph, the illustrious spouse of the same Virgin; in the name of angels and archangels; in the name of thrones and dominions; in the name of principalities and powers; in the name of virtues, cherubim and seraphim; in the name of patriarchs and prophets; in the name of holy apostles and evangelists; in the name of holy martyrs and confessors; in the name of holy monks and hermits; in the name of holy virgins and of all God's saints."

Father Smith was still praying away when the door opened and Mrs. Flanigan and two of the girls entered and knelt with him round the bed, crossing themselves mightily. "Into Thy hands, O Lord, I commend my spirit," Father Smith began, but the stripes on the old sailor's pajamas were going too quickly up and down for him to be able to answer, so Mrs. Flanigan and the two girls had to answer for him: "Lord Jesus, receive my soul."

Although the old sailor was too ill to be able to pray, Mrs. Flanigan said that she thought that it would be a good idea if he were to hold a crucifix in his hand, so that his eyes might get accustomed to the image of his Savior before meeting Him face to face in the next world, and Father Smith said that he quite agreed. So they took the crucifix from the bed-table and pressed it into the old sailor's hands. At first he didn't seem to want to hold it, but at last he gripped it firmly, and his eyes shone brightly and eagerly, and Father Smith told Mrs. Flanigan that he was sure that the old sailor was going to make a good death after all, and that he hoped that it would be a lesson to them all to forsake their sins, because Almighty God didn't always grant such wonderful last-minute graces.

The stripes on the old sailor's pajamas began to go up and down more quickly, and Father Smith shot out invocations at such a rate that Mrs. Flanigan and the two young ladies were unable to keep pace with him: "Saint Joseph, pray for me. Saint Joseph, with thy Blessed Virgin Spouse, open to me the breast of divine mercy. Jesus, Mary, Joseph, I give you my heart and my soul. Jesus, Mary, Joseph, be present with me in my last agony. Jesus, Mary, Joseph, let me sleep and rest in peace with you." Then the old sailor's pajamas were very still, and his face seemed to shrink away and away as though it were trying to become a baby's face again. Father

Smith prayed to the saints of God and to the angels of the Lord, that they might come and run thither and carry the old sailor's soul into the sight of the Most High, because he knew that the old sailor was dead.

More trams were running when the priest got back out into the street, all covered with red and blue and green advertisements, as though eating toffee went on forever, and the young men were out with their pale pink young ladies. Father Smith walked home because he was no longer in a hurry and because he wanted to think of the old sailor being judged by the Lord and to pray for him.

At the bleak corner of a street, round the South African War Memorial, clots of working men in stiff blue or brown suits and stiffer tweed caps stood with their hands thrust glumly into their pockets, because there were no racing or football results to discuss. In front of their sightless mooning, a handful of women and elderly men were gathered round a harmonium, which a young girl with pink rims round her eyes was pounding ecstatically. Just so, Father Smith reflected, as he stopped for a moment to observe, must Saint Paul have appeared to the inhabitants of Pamphylia and Phrygia and Ephesus and Corinth, only his doctrine must have been slightly less emotional, and of course there could have been no harmonium. He wondered whether, after all, Catholics might not learn from Protestants, and whether the precursor of real religious conversion in Britain might not be the revival of an order of itinerant preaching friars who would go about the lanes and the highways and the ugly cities preaching to everybody the great lovely truths about Jesus Christ and His Church. Of course there would be blasphemy and offense, but there would also be some gladness in the lives of those who listened and understood. As he stood there thinking this, a thick, burly little man with an enormous bowler hat and an inflamed eye detached himself from the hymn-singing group and accosted the priest.

"So you're Father Smith?" he asked truculently.

"I am. And to whom have I the honor of speaking?"

"You're speaking to Councilor Thompson, Chairman of the Protestant Action Society. I'm warning you: I'm your enemy. We don't want any dirty Catholics in this part of the town. We don't want them carrying on their blasphemous activities in the fruit market. And if you'll no get out, we'll make you."

For a second or two the priest thought that the man was going to spit in his face, but when he had uttered his threats, he walked quickly back to the hymn-singers, bulging beneath his bowler hat. Father Smith stayed on just long enough to make people think he wasn't afraid and then moved on homeward, unhappy within, because he didn't like being hated, not even for our Lord's sake. He had always wanted to be a popular priest; loved by his parishioners, with the religion he preached respected and understood by all. In his wiser moments he knew that this was a weakness, because God hadn't intended religion to be easy for anybody, least of all for priests. Such a moment came to him now as he asked God to give him strength not to be a coward. After all, he thought, God let modern priests off fairly lightly, since He didn't ask them to be grilled alive like Saint Lawrence. But perhaps being grilled alive hurt less than one imagined if one had God's good grace to help one. Then he remembered that, although it was already past two o'clock, he hadn't yet said his daily prayers for the conversion of Scotland, and he said them right then so that he could start straight away into his roast beef as soon as he reached home.

II

THE BISHOP LIKED a sausage for his lunch and maintained that nobody in the whole diocese could cook one as well as he himself did, not even the Jesuits, who had a lay brother who was a real dab at the job. Father Smith explained this tactfully to his landlady on the day that his lordship was due to lunch at the priest's lodgings, prior to accompanying him to the station to meet the Sacred Heart nuns who had been expelled from France. At first Mrs. Walsh said that she had never heard of such an idea: a holy bishop, who could consecrate and ordain, cooking his own sausage; but she gave in when the bishop himself arrived in his worn old overcoat with the top button almost off and smiled at her out of his clear twinkling eyes so blue beneath his thatch of white hair. She said that, faith, if his lordship would allow her to sew the button on his overcoat, she would allow his lordship to cook the sausage, only it wasn't to be just one sausage, but three at the very least, because an important man like a bishop needed to eat a lot and be strong so that he could carry out his great and wonderful work. So they all went into the kitchen together, and Mrs. Walsh sat down and sewed the button tight on his lordship's overcoat, and the bishop stood over the frying pan and explained to them both that the reason most people didn't cook sausages properly was that they forgot to keep turning them round.

The bishop and Father Smith did not talk much during lunch because the sausages were so good and because they had not much time if they were to be at the station in time to meet the French nuns when they arrived at two fifteen. The bishop was forty-seven years old, and he had been a bishop for the past three years, because the pope liked having young bishops in that part of Scotland, where the parishes were scattered and separated by sea, mountain, and loch. The bishop liked Father Smith and Father Smith liked the bishop, but they did not often meet, because his lordship was always traveling about in trains and boats, preaching and administering Confirmation in distant valleys and dells.

They had decided to take a tram to the station because the diocesan funds wouldn't run to cabs both ways, and anyway, it was a different matter ordering cabs for holy nuns, but our Lord was fully justified in expecting hale and hearty priests to travel less luxuriously, if not to walk on their legs. As they waited by the lamppost that said "Cars Stop by Request" and "Fire Plug 50 yds." and "Please do not Spit on the Pavement," the bishop asked Father Smith if he had heard the rumor that King Edward VII had been to Lourdes and knelt during the procession of the Blessed Sacrament. Father Smith said that he had heard all sorts of rumors about King Edward VII, but never one quite like that, and the bishop said that he knew what Father Smith meant, but they must both remember that kings and princes were exposed to much severer temptations than ordinary men and that it would be very wonderful indeed if Almighty God were to convert King Edward to the Catholic religion, because it would certainly do a lot of good.

When their tram came swaying along, the bishop stepped by mistake on a metal plug that the driver had forgotten to remove when he changed ends at the terminus, and there was a lovely inconsequent sound just like the sacring bell at Mass and really quite appropriate, Father Smith said. They went inside because it wasn't worthwhile going up on top for so short a distance. Father Smith was pleased to find that it was James Scott who was the conductor, and he introduced him to the bishop, explaining all about the new baby and about how Mr. Scott went to the depot every morning very early so that he might sprinkle his tram from end to end with holy water before the day's work began. Mr. Scott blushed a little when Father Smith said this, and Father Smith supposed that this must be because there were Protestants listening who wouldn't understand, and he thought, what with human respect and one thing and another, how very much more merit a layman like James Scott must gain for leading a good life than himself and the bishop.

But Mr. Scott couldn't stand talking for long, because he had to be handing out his white and blue and red tickets. As he moved away down the aisle, punching and pinging, the bishop began to talk about liturgical and formal prayer. Father Smith sat with his hat on his knees, because he did not think it polite to sit in front of a bishop with his head covered, even in a tram car.

People were wrong to condemn liturgical and formal prayer, the bishop said, because it was only courteous to God to think about what you were going to say to Him before you said it. Whereupon Father Smith said that he thought the critics of liturgical prayer condemned it because repetition tended to make it meaningless, with the result that sinners could murmur Hail Marys with their lips while planning further misdemeanors in their minds.

"I wonder, though, if they are quite right," the bishop said out above the booming and the zooming of the tram. "It seems to me that even the hardiest sinner cannot utter the sheer poetry of the Church's prayers without having his soul in some way ennobled by their lovely sound. Moreover, the *Pater* and the *Ave* are earth's sweetest greeting to Heaven, and only a vain man would imagine that he could frame a more beautiful. And whenever I look out on the hideousness and harshness of our industrial cities, I thank Almighty God deep down in my heart for having given His Church so many exquisite rites and ceremonies. For it is not bread and circuses that the people require, but poetry and prayer."

"'Poetry is the phrase that the young man murmurs in his heart; all the rest is only literature.' I remember reading that in a magazine once," Father Smith said.

"That's true as far as it goes, but it does not go far enough," the bishop said. "When young men murmur poetry in their hearts, they are looking for God, even though they may not know it. It is poetry that is a reflection of religion, not religion of poetry."

Father Smith could see that people were beginning to stare at the bishop and himself, popping at them hard, glittering, hating eyes, like the soda-water bottle stoppers you pressed down with your thumb. He knew, however, that they were staring only because they were so accustomed to hearing people say things that didn't matter that they were shocked when they heard people say things that did. If the bishop and himself had been talking about steel shares or the price of jute, nobody would have looked at them at all, but because they were talking about the things that alone gave meaning to life, their words aroused hatred, anger, and contempt. The priest thought sadly about all the talking that there was in the world each day—about the wind and the rain and golf and Aunt Maggie's new dress—and he thought, too, about all the important things that never seemed to get said.

"Probably your lordship is right," he said, more loudly than was necessary, because he wasn't going to be shamed out of talking about the things of God just because a tramload of worldlings was staring at him. "After all, our Lord and the saints have hammered out and chastened the holy phrases, so perhaps there is a grace to be found even in their echo."

The Right Reverend Monsignor Canon O'Duffy, administrator of the pro-cathedral, was already on the platform when they arrived at the station. He had been invited to meet the French nuns too, but because he was making a bee line for the gentlemen's lavatory, the bishop and Father Smith pretended not to see him but stood and examined the literature exposed on the bookstall, which seemed to be very, very worldly, although the bishop was pleased to remark that there were cheap editions of books by Robert Hugh Benson. There was also a new novel out by a young man called Hugh Walpole, and while the bishop and Father Smith were wondering who he could be, Monsignor O'Duffy came back from the gentlemen's lavatory and joined them. Monsignor O'Duffy was a great ape of a priest with coarse hair and a great hunk of face like a miner's, who poured his tea into his saucer to cool it and blew his nose on a red handkerchief at chapter meetings.

"Having a wee free read at the books, I see?" the monsignor greeted as he joined the bishop and Father Smith. "Afternoon, your lordship."

"Father Smith and I have just been having a most interesting discussion on poetry," the bishop said.

"Poetry's all blether," the monsignor said. "A lot of nonsense about 'love' and 'dove' and I don't know all what, and often it's downright sinful. Give me football for the lads any day of the week. And as for the lassies, they can sit by the fireside and do a bit sewing and be very much better for not bothering their heads about all yon highfalutin' rubbish."

The bishop and Father Smith saw that it was no use pressing the subject of poetry any further with Monsignor Canon O'Duffy, so Father Smith said that he wondered whether any of the nuns spoke English and hoped that they did, because his French was beginning to get rather rusty, which wasn't quite true because he rather prided himself on his French. Monsignor O'Duffy said right out that it was no use counting on him for any of the parlez-voo business, but the bishop said that he had spoken quite a lot of French in his day, because he had been at Saint Sulpice before he had been at Valladolid and had had to read aloud in the refectory. Father Smith was rather disappointed to hear this, because he wouldn't have minded being the only one able to do the talking, but he mastered his dissatisfaction quickly, because he knew that it was unchristian.

Far away out along the bend of the railway line, at the junction of the golf course and Sir Dugald Ippecacuanha's estate, a puff of smoke appeared above the trees, and a miniature worm of train rolled tinily along the embankment. Father Smith had often seen the puff of smoke at the same time and in the same place, and each time that he saw it, he sent a spiral of thanks up to God for having ruled even the world with the rhythm of liturgy and for keeping all the other safe old trees on earth still in their same safe places. "J'ai, tu as, il a," Monsignor O'Duffy began to recite with heavy humor. "Avez-vous vu la plume de ma tante," but the bishop interrupted him by reminding him that it was the first-class carriages that always stopped in front of the bookstall, and that they had better move further along the platform, because the good and holy French nuns would be sure to be traveling third.

The bishop was right. The nuns were traveling third-class and at the very end of the train, next the guard's van. Monsignor

O'Duffy, as he grunted along to meet them, said that he had noticed that nuns always travelled in the back of trains, and Father Smith said that that was perhaps because they were so mindful of our Lord's saying that the last in this world should be the first in the next. The nuns smiled when they saw the three priests, and the three priests smiled back. The bishop took off his hat and uttered the little speech that he had been rehearsing since Septuagesima: "Bon jour, ma Révérende Mère. Je suis enchanté de faire votre connaissance. Permettez-moi de vous souhaiter, ainsi qu'à toute votre communauté, la bienvenue sur la terre d'Ecosse." Father Smith said, "Je suppose que vos bagages se trouveront dans le fourgon" and Monsignor O'Duffy said, "Oo là, là, oui, oui," at which the Reverend Mother laughed.

There were eight nuns in all, and they stood with the wind blowing pretty pillows of pattern into their habits while Reverend Mother introduced herself and them. Father Smith didn't catch all the names, because they were French and Reverend Mother said them so quickly, and because he was too busy admiring the nuns' sweet, happy, holy faces to pay much attention. Two or three of the nuns were young, with such lovely, rosy cheeks and strong, white teeth and bright, blue eyes that Father Smith wondered why on earth the French had wanted to get rid of them, because they must have looked so lovely walking along old, cobbled streets.

The nuns apologized for having brought so much luggage with them, but they said that they couldn't have borne to have left all their beautiful candlesticks and vestments behind, especially the red chasuble that had once been worn by the Curé d'Ars. The bishop said that he quite understood this and that they had done quite rightly, because Almighty God would be more honored by beautiful things being used in His service in Scotland than by having them left behind in France, only he didn't say it very quickly, because he hadn't had since Septuagesima Sunday to practice it over in French. A bevy of large-striped stockbrokers in blown-out plus fours with brassies and cleeks glared at the nuns as they passed, but Monsignor O'Duffy glared back even harder, and the stockbrokers moved on, staunch Protestants who were willing to do anything for their religion except go to church.

While Monsignor O'Duffy and Father Smith were seeing about the luggage, the bishop explained to the nuns that they must expect to find their religion hated just as much in Scotland as in France, although less accurately. The reason for this, he said, was that the enemies of the Church in France had had the gospel preached to them but had rejected it, whereas in Scotland men scoffed and reviled through prejudice and ignorance. Reverend Mother said that she quite understood this and that she was sure that the other nuns understood it, too, and that they would all pray a lot for Scotland, that God might give it back the blessing of Faith.

The bishop and Father Smith had ordered only two cabs for the nuns, because they hadn't known that there was going to be so much luggage, but Monsignor O'Duffy managed to collar a third, because the driver was a member of the pro-cathedral parish, although he hadn't made his Easter duties for the last five years, at least so the monsignor said. Reverend Mother and the bishop and Monsignor O'Duffy all got into the first cab, and four of the nuns into the second, and only three into the last, because they had to take the box containing the red chasuble that had once been worn by the Curé d'Ars inside with them, as they couldn't very well trust it up front with the cabman on top, especially when he hadn't been to Holy Communion for so long. As the cabs moved off, a gang of hooligans who had been standing watching in front of a railway poster for Devon, Glorious Devon, started to jeer; but the bishop told Reverend Mother that she mustn't worry about that sort of thing, as the oafs and loungers who were yelling didn't really hate the doctrines of the Church about our Lord and the Blessed Sacrament but only the garbled distortions that ignorant men had represented to them.

As they rolled down through the town, the bishop asked Reverend Mother if she had ever been to Rome, and Reverend Mother said that she had but that she hadn't been as impressed as she had imagined and that she was sorry to say that some of the princes and high prelates of the Church hadn't seemed to have very spiritual faces and had hurried through even the holy mysteries of the Mass in a distraught and irreverent manner. The bishop said that that was perhaps because the Saxon mind could think of only one thing at once, whereas the Latin mind could think of several, so that it was possible that an Italian cardinal's eyes and face might reflect the worldly thoughts of half his mind, whereas the other half was really and truly thinking about our Lord and all that He had done for us. He said that he had noticed the same thing about British and continental soldiers: British soldiers looked as though they meant their drill, whereas continental soldiers slopped about in a most unmilitary manner, so that there was, curiously enough, a psychological connection between two such entirely dissimilar ceremonies as a High Mass in Westminster Cathedral and a full-dress parade of the Argyll and Sutherland Highlanders. Reverend Mother said that there was perhaps something in what the bishop said, but that his lordship must not forget that she herself was a Latin and no Saxon and that in spite of that fact she had been considerably shocked by the scurried ceremonial and the slothful thought of some of the higher clergy in Rome. Monsignor O'Duffy said, "Oo là, là, oui, oui," and everybody laughed a lot, although deep down within themselves, they were all quite pained that the higher clergy in Rome didn't look more spiritual.

Father Smith said that what they had just been talking about reminded him of a story about a Frenchman who had gone to confession and accused himself of not having been impressed by what he had seen in the holy city. "Ah, mon enfant," his confessor had said, "il vaut toujours mieux ne pas visiter la cuisine du Bon Dieu." The bishop laughed so much at this story that Monsignor O'Duffy wondered if he was ever going to stop, and he was rather irritated when his lordship went on for so long, because he himself hadn't understood a word, although he had said, "Oo là, là, oui, oui."

But if Monsignor O'Duffy didn't know French, he knew Italian, which he had learned at the Scots College in Rome. For although he had an Irish name, the monsignor had been born at Tobermory. There was once, he said, when the bishop had finished laughing, an Italian priest who had to preach a sermon on the feast of the patron saint of his native town, San Pietro di Buonarotti. "San Pietro Damiano fu un buon' santo," he began, "San Pietro di Roma fu un excellentissimo santo, ma San Pietro di Buonarotti, phew, che santo, amici miei!"

They were all still laughing at Monsignor O'Duffy's story when the cab drew up in front of the house that the nuns had had bought for them while they were still in France and that they were later going to convert into a school. Father Bonnyboat, of the Church of Our Lady, Mirror of Justice, Gormnevis, who had been entrusted by the bishop with the purchase of the new convent, was on the doorstep to greet them. He held in his hand a parrot in a cage, which he presented to Reverend Mother with a stiff little bow, saying "Oiseau, oiseau," and explaining that he had had the bird for five years and that it could say both "Dominus vobiscum" and "per omnia saecula saeculorum," but that it was with the greatest pleasure in the world that he presented it to Reverend Mother. Reverend Mother seemed rather embarrassed by the gift, and for a moment or two, Father Smith was afraid that she was going to say that the rule of her order forbade herself or her nuns to keep parrots, however holy their cluckings; but in the end, she thanked Father Bonnyboat prettily enough, and then they all went in to tea.

The nuns sat at a long table in the bare room that Father Bonnyboat had had prepared as a refectory. Reverend Mother did the pouring-out, and the bishop insisted on handing round the scones, even to the priests, because he knew that the highest title of the highest of bishops was *Servus Servorum Dei*, the Servant of the Servants of God. Father Bonnyboat had wanted to provide a little holy reading aloud during the meal, but the only French books he had been able to lay hands on were by Anatole France and Emile Zola. The bishop had said that they weren't quite suitable and that Father Bonnyboat could make up for this lack of edification in his sermon in the chapel afterward.

"Aiméz-vous les scones écossais?" Father Bonnyboat asked a young nun.

"Oui, ils sont délicieux, mais je crois qu'à l'avenir il va falloir nous contenter d'une alimentation plus austère."

"Quelquefois en Ecosse on a des kippers à son thé," Father Bonnyboat said.

"Oo là, là, oui, oui," Monsignor O'Duffy said with his mouth full.

As soon as tea was over, they all went into the chapel, which Father Bonnyboat had installed in the old billiard room. A small, wooden altar had been erected, and the Blessed Sacrament was reserved, with a red lamp burning in front. The bishop had previously blessed the billiard room quite thoroughly, saying that he thought this especially necessary, because the house had previously belonged to a chartered accountant. When they had all prayed a little, Monsignor O'Duffy sat down at the harmonium and wheezed out "Je suis Chrétien," which the nuns all sang with low, clear voices, and the priests didn't sing at all, because the nuns sang so beautifully.

When Father Bonnyboat stood up to preach, the bishop was afraid that the priest was going to yell out the customary rant that he kept for big occasions, "My dear brethren in Jesus Christ, none of you will ever wake up in Heaven wondering how on earth you've got there," because such a sermon would not have been kind to nuns, who had every reason to hope for salvation. Instead, the priest preached a sensible little sermon on sanctity, and in English too, because he couldn't get his subjunctives right in French, so he said. The world was wrong to laugh at saints, Father Bonnyboat said, because the production of a saint was God's highest handiwork. To be a saint didn't mean being a weak namby-pamby creature who couldn't say boo to a goose; to be a saint meant loving God with one's whole heart and one's whole mind and doing, thinking, and saying all things to His greater glory. That was the only philosophy that could save the world, but it would never save the world, because God Himself had said that His Kingdom was not of this world, but that did not mean that monks and nuns and priests were wrong in trying to be saints themselves and in encouraging others to try to be saints too. Our Lord Himself had said that many were called but that few were chosen, and that the vast supernatural machinery of the Church would have been worthwhile if in all time and space it had succeeded in producing only one saint. In the eyes of God, it was the invisible victories in the human soul that mattered and not the great splashing news in the papers about politics and Sir Thomas Lipton's yachts. When Father Bonnyboat had finished, Monsignor O'Duffy began to play the organ again, and the bishop, Father

Smith, and Father Bonnyboat went out to vest for Solemn Benediction of the Blessed Sacrament.

Father Smith always loved the service of Benediction, because it was so beautiful with our Lord there, all white in the center of the monstrance, and he sometimes wondered why lay-people wanted to go to concerts and theaters at all, when they could have so much more pleasure praising and adoring God this way. It was beginning to get dark when, as deacon, he took the Host out of the tabernacle, and the only lights in the chapel were the candles on the altar, which glowed like stars. In the tender smudge of darkness, the nuns knelt and sang lovely words, so that even Monsignor O'Duffy's chunk of face looked holy as it hung like a raw red moon above the keys of the harmonium. The nuns sang the *O Salutaris* and the Litany of Our Lady, and Father Smith thought that he had never heard any sound more exquisite than the syllables of "speculum justitiae" as they came clear and sweet from those invisible French lips. Then the nuns sang *Salve Regina* and the *Tantum Ergo*, and the bishop raised the Blessed Sacrament in the monstrance and made the sign of the cross high up over the kneeling nuns, stretching his arms away out, as though he were trying to bless all the sinners that there were in the world as well. The nuns sang the *Laudate Dominum* at a pious little gallop while Father Smith put the Blessed Sacrament back in the tabernacle. Then they all sang over again, "Adoremus in aeternum Sanctissimum Sacramentum" among the wreaths of incense, and the bishop and Father Smith and Father Bonnyboat left the chapel in their rich, white vestments.

Reverend Mother and the nuns all wanted to come to the door with the bishop and the priests to see them off and to thank them for their kindness, but the bishop pointed out that the climate of Scotland was much more rigorous than that of France and that their goodbyes could be said just as well in the hall. Reverend Mother said that it was "très, très gentil de la part de monseigneur l'évêque et de messieurs les curés de s'être donné tant de mal pour de pauvres religieuses réfugiées," and the bishop said that it had been no trouble at all, and the nuns said, "Mais si, mais si," and Monsignor O'Duffy said, "Oo là, là, oui, oui," and everybody laughed a lot, including his lordship the bishop.

Father Smith realized that there was trouble afoot as soon as the door of the convent had closed behind them, but he pretended not to see, as he walked with the bishop and the other priests, the blobs of hating faces strung like bladders along the outer railing. He tried also not to hear the ugly things that they were shouting, because he knew that our Lord wanted Catholics to be brave and to suffer for His Name's sake as well as to adore Him in beautiful chants, and because he knew that he wasn't brave and didn't want to suffer the least little bit. Then he looked at the bishop's serene face and Father Bonnyboat's surprised frown and Monsignor O'Duffy's jutting jowl, and he remembered all the saints, virgins, confessors, and martyrs who had endured so much for the love of Christ. "Passio Domini Nostri Jesu Christi," he murmured and knew no more as the sharp stone hit him on the temple and he fell, unconscious, to the ground.

III

THE ONLY TIMES that Father Smith remembered being really happy out of church during the last fifteen years had been when he was traveling in trains; but lying recovering in the hospital was almost as good, because, as in the trains, he had nothing immediate to do. The bishop had insisted on his having a room all to himself, and the Protestant nurses were very kind, although they kept asking questions about why Father Bonnyboat had always to be popping in every morning to give him Holy Communion.

He had reason to feel happy, too, because the whole town had been shocked at the news of the assault that had been made upon the bishop and the other priests and himself, and contributions were beginning to flow in for his new church. Even Protestants were subscribing. Sir Dugald and Lady Ippecacuanha had each sent a check for a hundred pounds. He was almost glad that that stone had made such a nasty cut on his temple now that the cause of religion had benefited so manifestly.

The novel that he was trying to read was called *Temporal Power*, by Marie Corelli. One of the nurses had lent it to him because she thought that Father Smith would be even nicer as a Scottish Episcopal clergyman than he was as a Roman Catholic priest and hoped that the book would convert him; but the priest found the book stupid and flamboyant, and he let it fall on the coverlet and lay back on his pillow.

Outside in the street, an invisible message boy passed, singing up into the blue and gold morning:

> "Anybody here seen Kelly,
> Kay-ee-double ell-wye,
> Anybody here seen Kelly,
> Kelly from the Isle of Man?"

The song normally amused Father Smith, because it made him think of Monsignor Francis Canon Kelly, vicar general and protonotary apostolic, who always gave himself airs when he deputized for the bishop and was allowed to sing pontifical High Mass in a white miter; but today he didn't listen, because he was thinking of the events of long ago that had moved him to become a priest.

He was never quite able to make up his mind whether it was the girl at the dance or the woman in the lending library that had first made him conscious that God was calling him. All that the girl at the dance had said was, "Kitty says that I'm sure to have a grand time at Ascot," and all that the woman in the lending library had said was, "Please give me a nice novel: something to while away the afternoon"; but both remarks had pierced the eighteen-year-old soul of Thomas Edmund Smith like nails and made him understand that Christ hadn't died sorely upon the Cross so that girls might have grand times at Ascot and the hairy-cheeked wives of successful solicitors while away long afternoons by reading drivel. He could still see the women's dresses reflected in pretty balloons of color on the ballroom floor, and he could still see the vast checked overcoat that the solicitor's horsey wife had been wearing, and stamped across them both, the knowledge that these easy, futile things were not for him.

From then on, he had been shocked by the dreadful realization that to the majority of people in the world, the spiritual, the search to correspond with the good and the beautiful thing, simply did not matter at all. Once, in a train, a great lout of a baboon-faced doctor had asked him, "What do you young men do with your spare time nowadays: booze or women or both?" Then young Thomas Edmund Smith, determined, at the risk of appearing a prig, not to deny from motives of human respect the truth that was in him, had answered, "I don't know, because I'm going to be a priest, you see." At which the doctor had laughed with enormous violent hatred and said, "What you want to do, young man, is to grow up." Well, if to grow up meant to condone the ugly things that made for man's huge unhappiness, Father Smith was glad to think that he had not grown up yet.

It had not been easy to become a priest, of course. It had not been easy to give up the soft, comfortable things of the world that were not sinful in themselves. Girls, too. Almighty God had made their lovely bodies, and it had not been easy to give up the hope of someday meeting a woman whose mind would be as beautiful as her hair; but nowadays, when he saw and heard the women he might have married yattering in public places, he did not think that God had asked such a tremendous sacrifice from him after all. And then when he had seen a few of them all wet and dripping in their bathing dresses, the practice of chastity did not seem quite as difficult as some of the saints had made out.

There had been, too, the tremendous consolations: the days begun, continued, and ended with prayer; the early morning Masses on weekdays in the seminary, with the world outside all cool and still before men got up to make it dirty again; the bishop who had ordained him saying in English, after the young priest had promised to obey him in Latin, "Thomas Edmund, me darling boy, I do believe you really mean it"; his first Mass, with his gray, quiet old mother at the altar rails, waiting to receive the Body of God at his hands.

His mother was dead now, buried by himself in the new cemetery on the mountainside. She who had first taught him to pray had seemed proud to be anointed by her own son, but Father Smith had felt very humble and very sure that the old lady was going straight to Heaven. He still felt humble when he thought of her and countered his occasional temptations to spiritual pride by the method that she had taught him and that she herself, so she said, had learned from an Irish Benedictine. "Always remember that you can't see into other people's souls, but you can see into your own, and so as far as you really know, there is nobody alive more wicked and ungrateful to Almighty God than yourself," she had said.

He tried her remedy now, lying back and praying with cool hands upon the cool sheets. He prayed for himself, because he knew that he ought to have been much holier than he was, because he was a priest. Then he prayed for the repose of the soul of Judas Iscariot, because he knew that even his case wasn't desperate, because God might have granted him the grace of final repentance as he fell from the tree. Then he prayed for Marie Corelli, because he thought she really ought to have known better and thought that God would think so too. Down in the street, another message boy began to sing, "Anybody here seen Kelly?" but Father Smith didn't hear him, because he had fallen asleep.

IV

FOR QUITE A few years now, Father Smith had always gone on
Saint Andrew's Day to say a prayer in the High Kirk, because the
church had once been Catholic and he thought that Saint Andrew
might like things better that way.

There was no one in the church except himself, because Protestants did not seem to use their churches on weekdays like Catholics, dropping in to say a wee prayer to our Lord between buying
the cabbages and seeing about the sultana cake. As he knelt there,
with the sun falling in through the stained-glass windows upon
the sheen of his old, black coat, Father Smith thought away down
the centuries back to the days when there had been a high altar in
the chancel. There the Augustinian monks had sung their daily
High Mass, and the passing of the hours had been rhymed on
God's wise, good clock of matins, lauds, prime, terce, sext, and
none. The *Salve Regina* had been sung at night among the shadows of the pillars, because the monks had thought that it was only
fit to make the same sort of noise in time as they would hear
throughout eternity.

These days had gone from Scotland now, and Father Smith
prayed that they would soon return, because he knew that only in

the poetry of faith could men find happiness and purpose. These days had gone from Scotland because men had been foolish enough to seek to reform from without instead of from within, failing to understand that a doctrine was not necessarily untrue because its adherents did not live up to its implications. And now the Blessed Sacrament and Mary and the Saints were gone too, and men and women were supposed to lead righteous lives without any of the helps that God Himself had instituted.

The priest was not so stupid as not to realize that there were many Protestants who led better lives than a lot of Catholics and who belonged to the spirit if not to the body of the Church because they had *animae naturaliter christianae*. Indeed, it sometimes seemed to him that God had made up to well-intentioned Protestants for the loss of the Faith, through no fault of their own, by allowing them to be better at loving their neighbors than Catholics were, although generally they failed to do so from supernatural motives. Catholics were, of course, better at loving God, and how should they not be, with the furniture of high Heaven itself to help them?

Yet it was no use, even out of respect for other people's most sacred feelings, trying to hide the fact that the Protestant heresy had done immense harm to the world at large, if only in securing the general acceptance of the misconception that belief was a corollary of virtue and that a man who beat his wife had no right to believe the Athanasian Creed. If it were true that faith was a privilege that diminished in geometric ratio to the practice of sin, Father Smith thought, then the hunters of foxes and stags would forfeit the right to believe in even one Person of the Trinity.

It all seemed quite clear to him as he knelt there, praying to Andrew and Columba and Kentigern and Margaret, that they should save Scotland for God again. A verger paused to look at him with enquiry and passed on, shaking his head, because he wasn't used to the spectacle of private devotion.

The minister himself was standing on the porch when Father Smith came out of the church. He was the Very Reverend Doctor James Gillespie, D.D., and he had once been Moderator of the General Assembly of the Church of Scotland. Father Smith always felt humble when he met Doctor Gillespie, because the minister always wore such smart, black tailcoats and was invited by the municipality to the opening of electric power stations and water-works when even his lordship the bishop was left out. To his surprise, however, the minister took off his glossy top hat as soon as he saw him and smiled most pleasantly.

"I'm very glad indeed to see you, Father Smith," he said. "I've been wanting to tell you personally how much I and my congregation deplore the disgraceful events of a fortnight ago."

"That is very kind of you, Doctor Gillespie, but I assure you that neither the bishop nor myself doubted for one instant ..."

They got on famously after that. Doctor Gillespie asked Father Smith what he was doing worshipping in the house of Rimmon, and Father Smith said that, as far as he was concerned, the High Kirk wasn't the House of Rimmon at all but God's old holy place, where he had come to say a prayer on Saint Andrew's Day. The minister looked a little unhappy when the priest said that, as though he knew what he had been praying for, and Father Smith understood that Doctor Gillespie wasn't really proud at all but was a large, unhappy man, anxious, like himself, that men should come in for Christ's wedding feast. As they walked down the street together, Doctor Gillespie said that it was braver of him to be seen abroad with Father Smith than it was of Father Smith to be seen abroad with him, because nobody would think that there was any chance of his converting Father Smith. Father Smith asked the minister whether the remark was intended as a compliment or an insult, and they both laughed, happy that they could unite in mirth if not in prayer.

V

IT WAS IN 1910 that the first cinema came to the town. Paolo Sarno took a chance on things and converted the old bus stables next his ice-cream shop, which was bang opposite the site on which Father Smith had already built the skeleton of his new tin church. The priest could see the advertisements from his presbytery window. They changed twice a week too, on Mondays and Thursdays: sometimes they were about a man called John Bunny and sometimes they were about two men called Gerald Ames and Stewart Rome, but the advertisement saying that afternoon tea would be served free of charge to patrons between three and four was always the same. People said that it was rather sporting of Sarno to be so enterprising, because the craze mightn't last any longer than the one for roller-skating in which the Italian had taken such a hard knock two years ago.

The canons of the chapter of the pro-cathedral, however, didn't think it sporting at all. They were perturbed because weekday attendances at Benediction of the Blessed Sacrament began to fall off, and the evening devotions in the month of May were performed only by the elderly, and even some of them hadn't been above popping in for an hour's Vitagraph and a wee free tea during the holy season of Lent when they thought none of the priests were looking. It was in vain that Monsignor O'Duffy had thundered from the pulpit, "It's no by sitting in red, plush airmchairs watching a lot of silly gowks sauntering and daundering about a lot of helter-skeltering moving-picture postcairds that any of ye'll ever see the bonny Bessed Virgin Mary face to face in the Kingdom of Heaven"; the attendances at Benediction during the month of the Sacred Heart were as poor as during the month of May. Some of the canons at the chapter meeting maintained that it would be more prudent not to condemn the cinema until His Holiness Pope Pius X had made an official pronouncement, but Monsignor O'Duffy had said that that was all havers and clavers and nonsense, and that if they had to wait on the official verdict of the Church, they might be argy-bargying till Doomsday, and that the Church had taken nearly nineteen hundred years to make up its mind about the doctrine of the Immaculate Conception, and that they couldn't afford to dilly and dally like that while young folk aye and auld folk, too, were walking straight into the jaws of Hell at sixpence a time and children half price.

It was decided, therefore, to send a deputation to attend a performance. This was possible because, as Monsignor O'Duffy pointed out, although local ecclesiastical law forbade priests to attend theatrical performances, the cinematograph was a very different cup of tea, indeed, and so could not be held to fall within the ban. He said, too, that if the members of the chapter didn't mind, he intended to go himself, as there was no cleric in the diocese who knew more about wickedness than he did, and that he would take his old friends the Reverend Fathers Bonnyboat and Smith with him, because it wouldn't be fair on Signor Sarno to be letting only austere and wise canons have a keek at his new-fangled toboggan slide down to the depths of the nethermost pit.

✠ ✠ ✠

Paolo Sarno seemed to have heard of their intended visit, for he was there in the vestibule to greet them, standing underneath a large, framed photograph of a lady called Flora Finch. Father Smith wondered why he hadn't come right out into the street, because that would have been even more polite, but Father Bonnyboat said that he mightn't have heard of their intended visit at all and that it was just by chance that he was standing there, and Monsignor O'Duffy said it was only because he couldn't very well have let them pay for themselves through yon wee hole in the wall into the lassie's face if he had come right out on the pavement, ha, ha. Anyway, there he was on the purple carpet, with his thick, light-brown fingers looking just like the advertisement for Palethorpe's sausages on the railway embankment.

"Buon giorno, reverendissimi signori," he greeted, because he thought that they all spoke Italian. The priests said "Buon giorno," back, except Father Bonnyboat, who had studied in the Scots College in Valladolid instead of the Scots College in Rome, and who said, "Buenos dias," instead. This made Paolo Sarno laugh and say: "Per Bacco! The reverendo father speaka the Italian like a Spanish cow, vero, no offense meant, reverendo father. You coma to see my show. Very good, very elevating, very pious. The reverendi fathers coma this way."

The reverendi fathers came this way, carrying their inverted black hats in front of their faces like soup-plates, and as they trooped along, Monsignor O'Duffy said to Paolo Sarno in a loud voice: "Wicked or elevating, shameful or pious, this new craze'll no last, Mr. Sarno, and in my opinion, you'd have done much better to open one of yon miniature shooting ranges with wee celluloid balls dancing about on jets of water, which are without the suspicion of sin."

It took Father Smith's eyes some little time to grow accustomed to the darkness, so that at first he seemed to be sitting in an immense black hole with Father Bonnyboat's overcoat on one side of him and Monsignor O'Duffy's overcoat on the other. Gradually, however, the darkness lightened to an amber haze in which he could make out lines of heads all about him like rows of chocolates in a box. On the screen, they were showing a blue river meandering along beneath green bridges and an old moldering church or two, which didn't seem to Father Smith very wicked, because the old moldering churches were almost certainly Catholic churches with the Body of God safe inside them, and a piano was playing away most politely, tra-la-la-la-la-la.

The same thought must have struck Father Bonnyboat, for he said across Father Smith to Monsignor O'Duffy, "Nothing very irreverent about that, Monsignor."

"Just you wait till we get to the acting," Monsignor O'Duffy said. "They tell me it's worse than yon machines you turn the handles on and look down on piers." He brought his ear very close to Father Smith's and whispered: "Tights. Tell him," he said.

But before Father Smith could pass this information on to Father Bonnyboat, a hat with a large pin stuck through it in the row in front of them turned round and said "Sssh," and Father Smith was left to wonder in silence how Monsignor O'Duffy knew so much about what was inside the machines you looked down and turned the handles on on piers. Then the piano suddenly stopped playing, and there was a noise in the air just like the buzzing the rotary brush made in the barber's, and the green bridges and the moldering old churches went on for a moment or two, and then they stopped too, and the lights went up, and the rows of heads in front of Father Smith had ears on them, and the screen turned out to be not a hung-up sheet at all but hard and rectangular and glossy, with high lights on it here and there as though the paint had run.

"Most edifying, really," Father Bonnyboat said.

"Just you wait, I tell you," Monsignor O'Duffy said.

The lights went down again. This time, the film was about a convict in prison. The convict wore a uniform striped broadly like a football jersey, and at first Father Smith was very sorry for him, because he seemed to be so miserable. But then the convict escaped and ran around a lot of street corners, and the policemen ran round a lot of street corners after him, but the convict always managed to escape, even when the policemen came at him from both directions at once, because he dodged behind doorways and the policemen ran into one another and knocked one another over. When Father Smith laughed, he knew he wasn't doing anything wrong, because he could hear Monsignor O'Duffy and Father Bonnyboat laughing too.

Then the convict ran along a beach, and there were a lot of pretty girls in bathing dresses eating chocolates on the sand, and the convict ran in among them and upset the chocolates, and Father Smith was wondering what Monsignor O'Duffy was going to say about the bathing dresses when down the gangway came a flashlight crying, "Chocleets, cigarettes, and matches." Then the flashlight turned into Angus McNab's face above two sprays of gold buttons leaning across Monsignor O'Duffy's waistcoat and saying to Father Smith, "Do ye no ken me, Father?" "One of my altar boys," Father Smith was going to explain to Monsignor O'Duffy, but up on the screen, the policemen and the convict and the pretty girls were throwing tarts and pies at one another's faces, and Monsignor O'Duffy was laughing too hard to be able to listen. The pie-throwing didn't seem very funny to Father Smith, and it didn't appear to strike Father Bonnyboat as very funny either, but the rest of the audience roared their heads off, and Monsignor O'Duffy laughed enough for both of them. "Yon fellow's a right comic and no mistake," he said as he sat wiping the tears from his eyes. Then he caught sight of a pretty waitress in a black frock and frisk of apron coming up the gangway. "Hi, lassie, what about yon free tea?" he asked.

"It'll be served during *Death or Dishonor*, sir," she said.

And served during *Death or Dishonor* their tea was, right bang in the middle of the Sheriff's speech, "Boys, I kinda reckon there's been dirty work at Red Gulch and we're going to put out that dirty skunk of a double-crossing horse-thief Ned Tranter's lights for him so that our God-fearing women folk can sleep safe in their beds o' nights and our maidens wander happy and careless 'neath a myriad stars," flashed across the screen just like that, without any commas, but with lots of dots at the end to make up. There was a tray for each, with a teapot and a cup and saucer and two hard little biscuits with ribs running along the back. Monsignor O'Duffy said that if the management had wanted to do things really well, they would have given them a boiled egg to their teas as well, but he seemed to enjoy the biscuits all right, soaking them in his cup of tea before he ate them and making great appreciative gurglings, champings, and suckings.

On the screen, above the cups of tea, Ned Tranter had captured the sheriff's pretty daughter, lassoing her while she was saying her prayers by her bedside and riding off with her on his horse to his mountain fastness. "Ned Tranter," she said to him in a great paragraph through her gag, "you may starve me, beat me, flay me, but never shall I consent to befoul God's great gift of love by becoming the mother of your children, nay, nor shall I cook for you, sew for you, dust for you. Death rather than Dishonor, Ned Tranter, for my heart belongs to clean-limbed Patrick Hogan of Lone Ranch." At this there was great cheering and clapping and stamping of feet, and Father Bonnyboat said that with a name like that, Patrick Hogan must surely be a Catholic, and Monsignor

O'Duffy said that that just showed ye that even on the fillums the great Holy Kartholic Churrch played a royal and triumphant rôle. Father Smith was too intrigued with the drama to say anything. With eager eyes and beating heart, he watched the sheriff and Patrick Hogan and the other boys of Red Gulch set out to rescue Molly Kintyre, whose eyes were like forest pools with the ineffable glory of the stars mirrored in their purple depths, at least that was what Patrick Hogan had said when he was playing snooker in a saloon bar with Mickey Riley.

As they set out on horseback, they all fired their pistols into the air to let Molly Kintyre know that they were coming, but of course Ned Tranter didn't hear, because he always slept with his dirty head under the blankets. Up hill and down dale they rode, firing their pistols all the time. Sometimes it looked very much as though they were riding up the same hill twice, but Father Smith was too excited to care. With the others he clapped, groaned, lost heart, and clapped again, but at last it was all over, and Molly Kintyre was restored to the arms of Patrick Hogan, who swore, colleen bawn, that he would never play snooker in saloon bars again, and the sheriff said, pointing his revolver at Ned Tranter: "Nix on the gunplay, Tranter. Put 'em up. You're cornered."

The three priests clapped with the rest of the audience, and Father Bonnyboat said that he hadn't seen anything so edifying for a very long time indeed, and Monsignor O'Duffy said that he was never afraid to confess when he was wrong, and that it looked very much as though he had been wrong in what he had said about the cinema, and that if the remainder of the program contained no unpleasant surprises, he would have to make amends to Signor Sarno by buying tickets for all the members of Saint Vincent de Paul Society.

There was, however, no remainder of the program, for as soon as the lights were lowered, the blue river and the green bridges and the moldering old churches started all over again, with the piano going tra-la-la-la-la-la and all. Father Bonnyboat said that he supposed that they really ought to be going, but Monsignor O'Duffy said that that was all havers and nonsense and that "continuous performance" meant that folks could stay in as long as they liked and that he was going to see yon bit again where they threw pies at one another, but that of course Father Bonnyboat and Father Smith could do what they liked. Even when, at the end of the blue river and the moldering churches, they flashed an orange notice on the screen, "Patrons who have seen the full program once are requested to vacate their seats in favor of those waiting for admission," even then he still held out, maintaining that it wasn't as though he were trying to get served with an extra free tea, but only that he wanted to see them fling yon pies again. But when he had seen them flinging the pies, he found that he wanted to see them setting out to round up Ned Tranter again as well, so they all stayed to the end of *Death or Dishonor* and tried not to think that the spectators standing up in the passage were staring at them.

"Of course, it's just a craze and it'll no last," Monsignor O'Duffy said when they stood outside again on the unenchanted pavement.

Father Bonnyboat said that he thought somehow that it was more than a craze and even wondered whether the blessed in Heaven might not be treated to a similar entertainment, since it was so uplifting; but Father Smith said that in Heaven the blessed would have our Lord to look at and that nothing could be more uplifting than that. Whereupon they all took off their hats, saluting the priesthood that was in one another, and went back to their churches, because it was the first Thursday of the month and they had confessions to hear.

VI

AT THE CONVENT, the nuns had hung the parrot that Father Bonnyboat had given them in one of the classrooms, because they thought that it would be elevating for the pupils to hear a parrot that made holy noises, especially as such birds weren't reputed to be pious. Mother Leclerc said, each time she heard the parrot say "Dominus vobiscum," that she felt sure that our Lord must have died for cats and dogs and birds as well as for men, but Reverend Mother told her not to be silly and that our Lord had died only for men, because it was only men who had immortal souls, and that if our Lord had died for cats and dogs and birds, why not for mice and rats and fleas as well? Mother Leclerc had said that, of course, Reverend Mother was right, but deep down in her heart she had cherished the hope that the parrot one day might sing in the heavenly choir with Saint John Chrysostom and Saint Cecilia and all the rest of them.

Father Smith said Mass at the convent on Sundays and Tuesdays and Thursdays, and Monsignor O'Duffy and Father Bonnyboat said it on the other days of the week between them, because the nuns were too poor to afford a chaplain of their own; but Father Smith was the only priest who went there to teach catechism, because he loved the nuns even more than the others did, and he liked talking to young children about God as well. The parrot had been put in the classroom in which Father Smith taught, but it said "Dominus vobiscum" only when he entered and "Per omnia saecula saeculorum" when he left and never interrupted at all in between.

When he was with children, Father Smith always found it easy to believe that God had made the world. They looked so fresh and pink and chubby that it was impossible not to see God's finger smoothing their youth. Of course, as the doctors of the Church and some of the high-up saints had pointed out, children could sin and willfully disobey God just as much as grown-up people, but the priest believed that children all started out in life loving Jesus naturally and became false to Him only through the itch of the senses or the fear of being thought more righteous than their fellows. When he had been a boy himself, Father Smith had longed to be grown up, because he had believed that it would be easier to obey our Lord as an adult than as a child, and he had been disappointed when he had found out that it was more difficult. He supposed that this was everybody's experience and that the great difference between priests and nuns and ordinary people was that priests and nuns went on trying.

There were boys as well as girls in the class to which Father Smith taught catechism in 1913, because, although the school was really a girls' school, the nuns taught small boys as well until they were seven. Elvira Sarno and Joseph Scott were both in the class. The Sarnos and the Scotts had had other children since, but Father Smith remembered Elvira and Joseph especially because he had baptized them both together on a rainy Sunday morning in 1908. On the blackboard above Father Smith's head was a statement, "Rubber was grown in Brazil before it was grown in Malaya," because Mother de la Tour had been teaching geography there half an hour previously, but the faces in front of the priest were too young to care, and Father Smith's face felt too old to care, and he didn't think that God cared either.

"What is sin?" he asked the rows of round, round faces through the scaffolding of dusty sunbeams that came crisscrossing in from the high windows.

"Sin is an offense against God by any thought, word, deed, or omission against the law of God," the round, round faces chanted back.

"How many kinds of sin are there?" the priest asked their sailor suits and the ribbons in their hair.

"There are two kinds of sin: Original Sin and actual sin," the sailor suits and the ribbons chanted back.

"Very good," the priest praised; and then suddenly he knew that it wasn't very good at all, because the children didn't understand what they were saying any more than the parrot did when he said, "Dominus vobiscum." They would have chanted, "Sin was grown in Brazil before it was grown in Malaya" with equal enthusiasm if they had been taught to do so. Sadly, he thought of all the children down the ages and through the climes to which the Church had taught their catechism and of how much wickedness there was still in the world, because wisdom had been learned only by rote and not hammered in with sharp words like new nails. Perhaps it was the priests who were to blame for the rottenness of things, because they themselves had not felt the raw meaning behind the smooth phrases with which they had sought to make others feel. Closing his penny catechism, Father Smith resolved that, however often the Message had been mocked and mauled, the children who now sat in front of him should understand and obey forever.

"There is just one thing I want you all to remember and I want you to remember it all the rest of your lives," he said. "It is what you learn in this classroom that matters most and will always matter. God sent you into the world to save your souls, and nothing else is important. When you are bigger, wicked men and women will perhaps try to make you believe that this is not so and that all that matters is to grow rich and powerful and be honored by your fellow men. This is not so. Remember always that God does not see as the world sees, and that a dirty, ragged tramp with the grace of God in his soul is infinitely more lovely and beautiful in our Lord's sight than any sinful monarch in his palace. Try to obey our Lord always. Remember that you may be right in your own soul when the whole world is wrong with its noisy tongue. People may try to tell you that religion is only for church and Sundays and that it is foolish to try to be a saint; they will be wrong: as this world and its pleasures will pass away, it is foolish not to try to be a saint, and one cannot be a saint without being religious all the week through. The toffee you tasted yesterday won't give you any pleasure tomorrow, but it may make you sick. Sin is like that; it is only pain and not pleasure that it will give you in the next world." He caught sight of Joseph Scott tugging Elvira Sarno's hair. "Joseph, what was the last word I said?" he asked.

"Please, Father, 'Original Sin and actual sin,'" the boy answered.

"Do *you* know, Elvira?" he asked.

"Please, Father, 'an omission against the law of God,'" the girl said.

"Please, Father, I know," another boy answered. "You were talking about what toffee would taste like in Purgatory."

The boys in the class were too young to laugh at this answer, but Father Smith saw that Reverend Mother was standing by the door and that she was laughing. "Per omnia saecula saeculorum," the parrot screeched, because as soon as Reverend Mother appeared he knew that it was the end of the lesson. Feeling slightly foolish, Father Smith left the dais and walked with Reverend Mother along the cool corridors of the convent out onto the green lawn at the back where the sun shone and Mother de la Tour was watering the flowers.

Father Smith had lots of holy relations in high places in the Church. He had a cousin at the Rota in Rome and another cousin who was a bishop in England and an aunt who was a Benedictine abbess, and they were all very pious and had very blue-blooded notions about loving our Lord and drinking soup out of their spoons sideways. Father Smith always felt very common and ordinary when he met them. He felt common and ordinary now as he walked in the garden with Reverend Mother, but not because she was a superior and he was only a humble priest, but because she had caught him out at trying to be cleverer than the holy men who had compiled the catechism.

Far away out along the bend of the railway line, at the junction of the golf course and Sir Dugald Ippecacuanha's estate, a puff of smoke appeared above the trees, and a miniature worm of train rolled tinily along the embankment, just as it had done five years ago when the nuns had first come to the town. The sight soothed Father Smith as it always did, and he realized that Reverend Mother couldn't really be laughing at him, because she loved our Lord just as much as he did and must have understood what had prompted his foolish zeal in the classroom.

"Cela se peut que vous avez raison, monsieur l'abbé," she said. "Perhaps it is a little our own fault that the world hates us so."

It usually amused Father Smith when Reverend Mother called him "monsieur l'abbé," but today it did not amuse him because she had so accurately measured his thoughts.

"Perhaps it is because we don't know the right way to be fanatics, ma révérende mère," he said. "And yet we must be fanatics if we are to teach the world all things which He has commanded us."

"Euntes ergo …" Reverend Mother said with a delicious accent. "No, monsieur l'abbé, we must not be afraid to be called fanatics, because fanaticism is only another name for acting logically."

Out on the main road, a surge of touts in tweed caps trudged to a football match. In the inside of their caps they had wire rings to make them look stiff, but they did not need any wire rings inside their faces. Looking at their red jaws all the same, Father Smith was suddenly afraid. There were so many people in the world, and most of them were so ugly that he could not understand how our Lord could love them. Then he caught sight of Monsignor O'Duffy trudging along with the touts and brightened because he realized that with God all things were possible.

"Il est bien brave, celui-là," Reverend Mother said as the monsignor took off his hat and waved a huge red handkerchief at them. "Football matches cannot be very wicked, if Monsignor O'Duffy goes to them," she added.

Father Smith agreed with Reverend Mother. His cousin, the bishop in England, would never have gone to a football match, although his lordship had once gone to a rugby international and boasted that he had been mistaken for an Anglican clergyman, which was a strange form of spiritual pride, because although the Anglican accent was all right, their doctrine was wrong and their orders invalid, as Pope Leo XIII had pointed out only the other day, in 1896.

"I'm afraid that you may have thought me a little foolish, speaking to the children like that just now, ma révérende mère," he said. "But I am convinced of one thing: unless we all try to be greatly good, we shall all be terribly bad, and it is by the practice of goodness alone that men will be saved from the material and spiritual consequences of this age of the machine. Perhaps you will laugh at me, ma révérende mère, but I cannot help thinking that it was exceedingly indiscreet of your fellow countryman Monsieur Blériot to have flown the Channel in that contraption of his."

"Voyons, monsieur l'abbé, pourquoi?"

"Because history shows that most human inventions tend to be used for evil rather than for good purposes. If I were Almighty God, ma révérende mère, I should not have allowed James Watt to watch that beastly kettle boil. And I think I should have silenced Marconi and Edison as well. For all these inventions defeat the main purpose of the Church: that man should be still and know that He is God."

"Perhaps you are a little right, monsieur l'abbé," Reverend Mother said. "Sometimes I, too, feel that there is a great calamity in store for the world. There must be something wrong when great countries like my country can banish those whose only crime is to serve the Lord zealously." A shining film came over her eyes as she spoke, and Father Smith knew that she was thinking about French villages with "Byrrh" and "Quinquina" painted on the walls of houses.

"Perhaps men don't learn better because God doesn't let them live long enough on earth," Father Smith said. "As soon as they have made a pretense of school, they have to be teaching their sons, and then their teeth go long and yellow and they are dead. It is the same with our civilization: things move too quickly. Men haven't ploughed enough fields to be able to work safely in factories."

"Poor France," Reverend Mother said. "And now, monsieur l'abbé, let us go and talk to Mother de la Tour about her flowers."

Father Smith wondered whether Reverend Mother was trying to rebuke him by changing the subject, but when he looked sideways up at her laughing eyes, all that he could see was the miniature black-and-white image of Mother de la Tour, bending patiently over her flower beds.

VII

ON GOD'S CLOCK it was the Feast of Saints Perpetua and Felicity, Martyrs, 1914, when Lady Ippecacuanha went snooping into Father Smith's new tin church to see how the building of the sanctuary was getting on. In her Donegal tweed costume and tackety golf brogues and with her monocle like a half-crown in her eye, she clacked up the aisle and entered a front pew, where she knelt with well-bred arrogance, for, although she was a suffragette and had set fire to the bookstall at Kincairn's Junction, she was a religious woman and believed that God was in most places, even in Roman Catholic churches. Kneeling there, she came to the conclusion that she rather liked the smell of incense, which was, after all, ever so much pleasanter a disinfectant than carbolic.

The sacristan, who now had a full-time job looking after the church and cleaning it, came out from putting fresh flowers on the Lady altar and saw her kneeling there. Mistaking her, by reason of her monocle, for a man, he came up from behind and tapped her on the shoulder.

"Take off your hat in the hoose o' God," he commanded.

With a jerk of her head, Lady Ippecacuanha turned her full frosty face and red hair upon him.

"Can't you see that I'm a woman?" she asked.

"Mormon or no Mormon, take off your hat in the hoose o' God," the sacristan commanded.

In the presbytery, Father Smith was sitting reading the *Catholic Trumpet*, which, as usual, was full of parish pump and diocesan drain. "Ne lisez jamais les petits journaux religieux," his confessor was reported to have counselled Baron von Hügel. As he read the holy bilge and sacred bunk, Father Smith could believe that the baron had been well advised. He was not able to think about this for long, however, for the front-door bell rang loudly and Lady Ippecacuanha came marching in just as though she were looking for a golf ball to hit with a brassie.

"Father Smith, I must ask you to dismiss that rude verger of yours immediately," she said, as flaming as her red, red hair.

Father Smith had met Lady Ippecacuanha twice in his life before: once when he had called at Glenclachan to thank her and Sir Dugald for their generous contribution toward his new church; and once at a nonsectarian charity concert where she had sung "Have You Ever Seen an Oyster Walk Upstairs?" and knocked a flowerpot over into the orchestra.

"Perhaps if you were to tell me exactly what the matter is," he suggested.

Lady Ippecacuanha told him briefly, bluntly, and blisteringly. She said that she had never been so insulted in her life. Observing a twinkle in the priest's eye as she spoke, she concluded with vehemence:

"I can see that you are amused, Father Smith; I am not amused, and I do not think that my husband will be amused either when I tell him what has occurred. I must say, however, that I am rather surprised at your attitude, because, in spite of the fact that you are a Roman Catholic clergyman, you have always impressed me as being a gentleman and not at all like some of your colleagues, that dreadful man Monsignor O'Duffy, for instance."

"My dear Lady Ippecacuanha," Father Smith began, praying quickly to God to help him because he *had* been amused and because Lady Ippecacuanha and Sir Dugald had each given a hundred pounds toward the building of his new church, "My dear Lady Ippecacuanha, I am sorry indeed if my sense of the grotesque has run away with me. For it is as grotesque that you should be mistaken for a Mormon as myself for a prizefighter, and I think that I should pardon you a smile, Lady Ippecacuanha, if I were indeed to be mistaken for a prizefighter. I cannot, however, dismiss my sacristan for such a misunderstanding, because he, after all, was only doing his duty, seeking to exact reverence toward our Blessed Lord in the Sacrament of the altar even from those whom he presumed to be ignorant of His presence. I cannot do it, Lady Ippecacuanha, even though you and your husband have been so generous to my church, and I cannot give you back your money, because it has all been spent long ago. And Roman Catholic clergymen are all God's gentlemen, Lady Ippecacuanha, in that they fulfill Cardinal Newman's definition of the term, as never wittingly wishing to do hurt to anyone. Monsignor O'Duffy may not see eye to eye with you and me on certain points of social etiquette, but he never smokes his pipe in God's drawing-room, which is a much more important matter. He has a big, free heart, and he loves our Lord with the simplicity of a little child. If he were to be mistaken for a Mormon or even for a tight-rope walker, I think that not only would he be amused himself, but that he would expect other people to be amused too, since his vocation as a priest of God is so plain for all to see." He did not look at Lady Ippecacuanha until he had finished making this speech, and when he did look, he was surprised to see that her eyes were full of tears and that her prominent, big, yellow teeth were sticking right out of her mouth like piano keys. "I am sorry, Lady Ippecacuanha," he said. "I assure you that I had no idea ..."

"There is nothing whatever to be sorry about, Father Smith," she said, smiling through her tears as she dabbed at them with a mighty handkerchief. "I am a wicked, proud, vain, arrogant woman, and I thank you for a most efficient lesson in humility." She thrust out a great paw at him as she spoke, and Father Smith, feeling rather foolish, shook it, because he did not see what else he could do.

As he accompanied her to the door, Lady Ippecacuanha began to talk about Father Bernard Vaughan and how she had heard him on two occasions in Farm Street and what a very fine preacher she thought him. Father Smith said that the Sunday on which the Jesuit had preached the first of his famous sermons on the sins of society had come to be known as the First Sunday After Ascot, and Lady Ippecacuanha, who was not very subtle, said that she wished the priest would pitch into golfers as well, because there were some dirty cads who smoothed down the sand in bunkers with their niblicks when they thought their opponents weren't looking.

As they stood on the top of the steps at the entrance to the presbytery, a surge of ragged, scruffy children came screeching and scampering up the street from the parish school. Some of them were barefooted and some were dirty and some of them had jammy rings round their mouths, but those of the boys who had caps on took them off as they passed the church, because they knew that Jesus was there in the tabernacle, and they took them off to Father Smith as well, and most of the little girls waved their hands. Seeing the involuntary expression of distaste sweep over Lady Ippecacuanha's rocky well-bred face and knowing that she was going to feel humble again a second afterward, Father Smith helped her by explaining:

"In this country, the Church is the Church of the poor, Lady Ippecacuanha, and on the whole I'm not sorry, since it tends to keep both clergy and people in the invigorating and spiritual and material conditions of primitive Christianity. In Scotland, our bishops are not asked to meet visiting princes or to exchange courtesies with diplomats, and so they accept their episcopal dignity as God intended that they should accept it, simply and humbly, as a duty rather than a privilege. And our layfolk, who know that it is easier for a camel to pass through a needle's eye than for a rich man to enter into the Kingdom of Heaven, accept their poverty as a proof of God's love and offer up their slavings, their ticket-punchings, and their scourings as a psalm to His greater honor and glory. They are not very clever, most of them, it is true, but both the stupid and the intelligent have always crowded out the Church of God; it is the half-educated who have always been too proud to come in." Thinking that he had perhaps gone too far, Father Smith was glad when Lady Ippecacuanha drew his attention to her husband, swaggering up the street with their fifteen-year-old son, who, it was obvious from a distance, had no jammy ring round his mouth.

Sir Dugald Ippecacuanha had a purple club-window face and smelled of Harris tweed, licorice pellets, and cigars. He had been a professional soldier for ten years but had retired from the army to manage his estate. His son was a golden boy who had already won his school colors for cricket.

"Father Smith's just been giving me a most salutary lesson in humility," Lady Ippecacuanha explained.

"Glad somebody's able to keep her in order, Father," Sir Dugald rumbled. "And to tell you the truth, I'm not altogether surprised that it should be an R.C. padre. Met a lot of them in the army, and they always struck me as being good fellows. You know, no nonsense about them. Didn't give a damn about religion any more than anybody else did. We had one with us in the mess at Delhi. Drank like a fish and played a rattling good game of polo."

Father Smith didn't quite agree that the characteristics that Sir Dugald had mentioned were essential qualifications of a priest, but he decided that he had done enough preaching for one morning, and besides, Sir Dugald was obviously trying to be kind.

"Looks as though there's going to be trouble soon," Sir Dugald said as Lady Ippecacuanha and he took their leave. "I don't like the look of Germany at all. Well, if it comes to the bit, I'll be ready enough to get into the scrap. Soldiering's a washout in time of peace, but it's grand in time of war. And perhaps Alistair'll be in it too. He's a sergeant already in his OTC at school. If it comes to the bit, every boy with grit'll long to be in it."

Father Smith could see that Lady Ippecacuanha didn't share her husband's enthusiasm, and he didn't share it himself, because he thought wars between nations could only hinder men from living as our Lord would have them live. When he went back into the presbytery, he found it difficult to begin his Office because Sir Dugald's words had disturbed him so much.

VIII

WHEN FATHER SMITH left for the front as a chaplain, the bishop insisted on accompanying him to the station. Monsignor O'Duffy and Father Bonnyboat had gone on ahead in the cab with the priest's luggage, because they knew that the bishop wanted to walk alone with Father Smith so that he could explain about Father Bonnyboat having been appointed to look after his parish during his absence. Quite a lot of soldiers as they passed saluted Father Smith because of his officer's uniform, and Father Smith saluted back, and the bishop took off his hat as well because he thought it was only polite.

"You see," the bishop began as they walked along the warlike streets with sailors lurching out of public houses and gaudy women in high-laced boots lurching out with them, "You see, you've been away from the Holy Name for nearly a year now, and Father Bonnyboat's curate at Our Lady, Mirror of Justice, is quite capable of taking over from him. And the Holy Name has become such a very much more important parish than Our Lady, Mirror of Justice, that I felt that only a priest with Father Bonnyboat's experience ..."

"Your lordship has no need to explain," Father Smith said. "I understand perfectly, and I assure you that I find the arrangement most reasonable."

"I was sorry that you should be among the first of my clergy to go, but I do not think that I should have willed it otherwise," the bishop said. "I cannot help feeling that a great and lasting spiritual good is going to come out of this war. How could it be otherwise with so many of our bravest and fairest and youngest dying so nobly for so great a cause? There is going to be a great opportunity for the Church of God after this war, Father, and those priests will best be able to take advantage of it who have known the comradeship and shared the hardships of the gallant men who shall make the world anew."

Father Smith did not know quite what to say, because although he wanted to agree with the bishop, he knew that the majority of the men with whom he served had no consciousness of fighting in a spiritual crusade. For one came to know men as much by what they didn't talk about as by what they did. The conversations in the anteroom and at the table of all the messes he had known had all been distressingly similar: Bruce Bairnsfather, Alice Delysia, George Robey, Phyllis Monkman,[1] a good time on leave, ready for another crack at the Hun. He had never heard anyone talking about the war being fought to usher in the Kingdom of Christ on earth, although the politicians and prelates in Parliament, press, and pulpit kept on asserting that that was indeed the case. But how could it be the case if the very men who were fighting the war were not fired with the same purpose? Indeed, did they not very often give the impression of being willing to go to almost any lengths to keep the Kingdom of Christ as far in the background as possible? If the war were not a

---

[1] Bruce Bairnsfather: British humorist and cartoonist of the First World War.
   Alice Delysia: stage name of Alice Henriette Lapize, French actress and singer who performed in English musical theater.
   George Robey: English comedian, singer, and musical theater actor.
   Phyllis Monkman: British stage and film actress.

crusade, then ought not His Holiness Pope Benedict XV to do something about stopping it, since there were pious, practicing Catholics fighting on both sides? Looking at the bishop's placid, peaceful, white hair creeping out from under his broad, black hat, Father Smith abandoned his perplexities. The war must be being fought for some good end if so holy a man as the bishop tolerated it, and Pope Benedict XV, deep in the panting heart of Rome, surely knew his own business better than any pernickety, quibbling parish priest. Then a large, empty-eyed, loose-mouthed floozy chewing chocolate at the entrance to a public house caught his attention, and Father Smith recognized Annie Rooney, a child of Mary who hadn't been to Mass for the last two years. The priest gazed at her appealingly, but the girl stared back rudely and then strutted off with a sailor. The bishop had been looking at the public house too.

"Perhaps public houses look more wicked from the outside than from the inside," he said.

"That unhappy girl is one of my parishioners, or at least she used to be," Father Smith said.

"Perhaps she looks more wicked from the outside too," the bishop said. "In any case, I shouldn't worry too much about her if I were you, Father. She may be like that just now, but once the war's over and righteousness enthroned, she'll be a good-living Christian like everyone else, or she will feel horribly unfashionable if she isn't."

When they arrived at the station, Father Bonnyboat was waiting for them by the big, new advertisement for Bovril. He took Father Smith by the arm and fairly lugged him onto the platform, where Miss O'Hara was waiting with a fair selection of her cock-and-hen choir and Monsignor O'Duffy, his tram ticket still stuck in the side of his hat, ready to conduct it. As soon as the bishop and Father Smith appeared, they broke into "Ecce Sacerdos Magnus," because although it was chiefly Father Smith whom they had come to honor, they couldn't very well forget the bishop, especially when he was always so kind and friendly to everybody and not the least little bit stuck up about being a bishop. Then, when they had sung their Latin, they sang their Scots: "Bonny Chairlie's Noo Awa." The tears came to Father Smith's eyes as he watched them, because he knew that it wasn't about Prince Charlie at all that they were singing but about himself, because he was leaving them and they didn't want him to go and were shy about saying so right out loud. Reverend Mother and Mother Leclerc and Mother de la Tour were there also, but they weren't singing, because it would have been wrong for nuns to sing secular songs in public, but Father Smith knew that down beneath their holy bibs their hearts were singing just as loudly as anybody else's. Then, far away out along the bend of the railway line, at the junction of the golf course and Sir Dugald Ippecacuanha's estate, a puff of smoke appeared above the trees, and the train that was to bear him away came rolling tinily along the embankment.

Monsignor O'Duffy stopped the choir at once and, mopping his brow with his red handkerchief, said, "I now call upon his lordship the bishop to make a wee speech."

"My dear children in Jesus Christ, we are gathered together today to bid farewell to one of our most beloved priests and pastors, the Reverend Father Thomas Edmund Smith, or perhaps I should say Captain Smith," the bishop began. Father Smith looked away from the bishop, because he knew that the bishop was looking at him and meaning every word he said. He looked at the bookstall, piled with Gene Stratton Porter's *A Girl of the Limberlost*, Jean Webster's *Daddy Longlegs*, and Nash's Magazine serializing *Saints' Progress* by John Galsworthy, but he couldn't help hearing some of the flattering things the bishop was saying. It all made him feel humble and rather guilty because he knew he wasn't really the saint the bishop was trying to make him out to be but an unworthy servant of his Lord who often lost his temper and let his mind wander during his prayers, which were things no really devout priest would ever do. Then little Elvira Sarno, who was nine now, stepped forward and presented him with a bouquet of roses, which she said were from the nuns and the schoolchildren and which they had picked from Mother de la Tour's garden, and might his thoughts of them be always as sweet. There was a great deal of clapping and Monsieur O'Duffy shouted "Speech!" and Father Smith somehow heard himself talking back at them, thanking them for their kindness and telling them about how good our Lord wanted them all to be, especially in time of war. Then Monsignor O'Duffy raised his hand again and they all sang "For He's a Jolly Good Fellow," and this time Father Smith was almost sure that he could see the nuns singing as well, although he supposed that they oughtn't to be. Then they all broke up and churned along in a crowd to pack him into his compartment.

The priest was rather shamed to be traveling first-class in front of them all, because he knew that none of them ever travelled first-class, not even his lordship the bishop when he was jogging about the Highlands on episcopal visitations, and he explained to the bishop and the nuns that it wasn't really his fault, but that there was a rule about it in the army. The bishop and the nuns said that they quite understood, and Monsignor O'Duffy said that he and the Vicar General had once travelled first-class for nothing from Kincairns Junction to Gormnevis because there had been no more room in the third-class carriages owing to the Sodality of the Sacred Heart and the Bona Mors Society both having their annual outings on the same day that year. Mother de la Tour said that she had never sat in a first-class carriage before, because she had always been brought up to believe that people who travelled in first-class carriages went straight to Hell when they died, and she asked Reverend Mother if she thought that there would be any sin in her trying the cushions just to see how soft they really were, and Reverend Mother said, "Puisque c'est comme ça, allez-y les essayer un peu." So in front of the eyes of a block-faced captain of artillery who was pretending to read *The Rough Road* by W. J. Locke, Mother de la Tour tried out the cushions and bounced up and down on them to the greater glory of God and cried through the open window that even in Paradise itself, cherubim and seraphim could desire no more comfortable choir stalls.

Then the bishop said that it was time for Father Smith to be getting into the carriage himself, because the engine had shunted round to the other end of the train and he could see the guard getting ready with his green flag. So Father Smith shook hands with them all and knelt down and kissed the bishop's ring, and the bishop gave him his blessing in a swift little Latin patter. Then Father Smith got into the carriage and shook hands with them through the window all over again. The captain of artillery in his corner looked more imperturbable than ever. Then the minister of the High Kirk and Lady Ippecacuanha both appeared from nowhere, and the minister said that although he had not the honor of belonging to the same great communion as Father Smith, he nevertheless wished him Godspeed and a safe return, and Lady Ippecacuanha said that Father Smith mustn't say a word to her husband, but she felt in her bones that she was going to become a Roman Catholic one of these fine days, which wasn't altogether as strange as it might sound because she had once known a countess who had been to Lourdes. Out on the platform, Monsignor O'Duffy raised his hand, and because they didn't know any more secular songs, the bishop and the choir and the nuns sang the

"Non Nobis, Domine," because they knew that they were not sufficient to think anything of themselves as of themselves but that their sufficiency was from God. They were still singing as the train moved away, and Father Smith's eyes were too full of tears to see the captain of artillery rudely staring.

IX

AS SOON AS he had shriven the boozy major, Father Smith wanted to get Holy Communion into him quickly before he could go out on the booze again, so he took advantage of the dispensation that allowed the faithful to communicate without fasting in the battle area. Along with a Portuguese private and two corporals of the Cameron Highlanders, the major knelt at the altar rails in the dark evening church at Noeux-les-Mines. Father Smith put on a white stole over his uniform and gave them Holy Communion, because they were all going up the line that night and might soon be blown into knowing more about Almighty God than the Holy Father himself.

The major had been educated at Ampleforth, but since then, he had racketed about a lot, although in argument with Father Smith, he always maintained that God was a Sahib in these matters and wouldn't send a chap to burn forever in Hell just because he had a bit of fun with the girls and the bottles. In his blander moments, Father Smith had felt inclined to agree with the major, because he had always held that the practice of Christianity was something more than the permanganate of burgess repression and that not everyone that said unto Him, "Lord, Lord, I have not slept with a pretty actress," should enter into the Kingdom of Heaven; but he never admitted this to the major for fear of stimulating his devotion to the popular sins. Instead, he had quoted Monsignor O'Duffy preaching on the feast of Saints Hippolytus and Cassian, 1911, to the whiskery members of the West of Scotland Catholic Needlework Guild: "Make no mistake about it, my dear friends: the pavements of Hell pullulate with liars, thieves, murderers, bibbers of gin, and fornicators; but far the biggest queue for the flames is that of the fornicators, worse by far than the biggest jam of folks you ever saw at a cup final."

When he had finished giving the major Holy Communion, Father Smith didn't walk back to headquarters with him, because he knew that that might make the major feel awkward after what he had just had to say in confession about the girl in Rouen. Instead, he stayed on to pray in front of the tabernacle with its curtains hanging white and still in the warm evening air. "O my God," he prayed, "make good come out of this war; make men as courageous in Thy service as they are in their country's; make women more demure but not less beautiful; mold their maidenhood upon Thy Blessed Mother's and place their feet in her pattern; calm youth to Thy contemplation; bless and increase priests and poets; root out from our hearts all love of eminence, comfort, and pleasure; confound wealth and destroy politics; and pour out Thy grace in tumbling rivers." He felt happier when he had prayed his prayer. Then he prayed for the old sailor whom he had shriven on his deathbed in 1908, in case he might still be in Purgatory. Then he prayed for himself, lest he mistake the wickedness of others for a reflection of his own excellence. Far away, the guns sounded like hills rolling, and Father Smith prayed for those who might even then be dying.

The French priest with the beard came in and knelt down a few chairs away. Father Smith always felt ashamed when he saw the French priest, because the French priest wasn't an officer like he was but a private soldier who had to march and muck and fight just like any other French soldier and all for next to nothing a day. Father Smith knew the French priest quite well, because they had used the same altar in the mornings for a fortnight now. They used the same vestments too, because the French priest always finished his Mass five minutes before Father Smith began his, and the curé of the parish didn't like his sacristan laying out two sets. The French priest stayed behind to hear Father Smith's Mass when he could, because he said that he found it even more devotional to hear Mass than to say it. When they came out of the church together, the French priest would talk for a little in the sun and the early morning ivy and then jump on his bicycle and ride back to his regiment, looking very ordinary; but Father Smith knew that it wasn't only because he was in a hurry but because he didn't want to compromise Father Smith by being seen walking through the streets with him when Father Smith was an officer and he wasn't.

This evening, the French priest didn't seem to have very long prayers to say, because he came out of the church at the same time as Father Smith. The ivy could no longer be seen because it was dark, but it could be smelled and tasted on the tongue, rich and damp and bitter.

"This time it's goodbye, I am afraid," Father Smith said.

"You mean you go away?"

"I am afraid I do."

"That is sad because I liked talking to you."

"I liked talking to you too." Father Smith felt that there was something terribly important that he ought to say to the French priest, something about how wonderful it was for them both to be priests together, ministers of the patience of Christ, toilers at the great effort, but the words wouldn't come and probably never could until they both met in Heaven. Instead, he said:

"Did I tell you that where I come from in Scotland there are French nuns?"

"Then when you will see them again, you will tell them from me that it will not be long before they will be back again in France," the French priest said. "Or at least I hope that it will not be long."

"I am sure of it," Father Smith said. "I am sure that in France as in Britain there will be a great return to religion as soon as the war has ended."

"Our Lord cannot fail to hear all these prayers," the French priest said. "And these so young boys when they will have died, they too will pray, and God will listen." He dropped suddenly on his knees before Father Smith. "Perhaps before you will go, you will bless me," he said.

"Benedicat te Omnipotens Deus, Pater, et Filius, et Spiritus Sanctus," Father Smith said, tracing the sign of the cross. "And now, monsieur l'abbé, perhaps you, too, will bless me."

They did not talk again when they had blessed each other but shook hands in silence, and each went his way. Father Smith walked back happily and humbly beneath the high scatter of the stars. When he reached headquarters, he found the battalion already fallen in, their steel helmets stamped like saints' haloes on the dark blue window of the sky.

"Well, and where the Hell have you been?" the colonel asked, but Father Smith knew that he didn't really mean it rudely, because although the colonel had often said that he had no use for parsons, he had also said that he didn't mind priests coming into the front line at all, because he knew that they had a special job to do.

When at length they moved off, Father Smith found himself side by side with the boozy major, but at first they didn't talk much, perhaps because the night was so beautiful. The marching men looked beautiful too, with their rows and rows of heads going on and on. From time to time, they sang the secular psalms that seemed to soothe their spirit: "There's a long, long trail awinding into the land of my dreams"; "You called me baby doll a year ago; you told me I was very nice to know"; "At seventeen he falls in love quite madly with eyes of a tender blue." Although he knew that there was no harm in the songs, Father Smith could not help feeling how very much more appropriate it would have been if they had sung psalms like the nuns sang, especially since they were fighting a righteous war. To cheer himself, he began singing to himself under his breath, "Montes exultaverunt ut arietes: et colles sicut agni ovium"; but somehow the words didn't rhyme to the rumble of "We are Fred Karno's army," and he gave it up. Instead, he let his thoughts slide along in lazy images and speculations. How very wonderful it would be, he thought, if he were to win the Military Cross. And the Distinguished Service Order. And the Victoria Cross. The colonel wouldn't ask him where the Hell he'd been then. The colonel would respect him then. And the bishop, how pleased the old man would be! And the nuns and Monsignor O'Duffy and Father Bonnyboat and all his parishioners. The send-off he got at the station would be as nothing compared with the welcome that he would receive at the same station when he arrived back with the three bright ribbons on his breast. They'd all be there to meet him, and the town council as well, and the nuns' eyes would be shining, and Monsignor O'Duffy would wave his huge, red handkerchief in the air and cry: "My lord bishop and folks, I now have great pleasure in calling upon ye all for to give three cheers for that great hero, the Reverend Father Thomas Edmund Smith, V.C., D.S.O., M.C."

Then with haste he chased the picturing from his mind, for he knew it to be sinful, because pride had made him seek honor and glory in dreams and because such visionings multiplied by a million produced much of the world's misery. He reminded himself of how he had vowed at his ordination that he would never seek advancement or preferment but would be Christ's doormat all the days of his life. This oath he now repeated silently within himself. A great happiness rose in him, because he knew again what Jesus had meant when He said, "He who loseth his life shall find it."

"I say, Father, do you mind if I ask you a rather theological question?" the boozy major suddenly asked. "Tell me: is it a sin to kiss a girl at a dance when you've no intention of proposing marriage to her?"

"That all depends on how the kissing's done," Father Smith answered.

"In other words, a chap mustn't get too much of a kick out of it?"

"I'm afraid not."

"That's what's laid down in the rubrics, is it?" The major didn't seem to expect an answer, for he added: "I must say, God's a bit hard on a chap at times. Still, in spite of what you say, I'm sure God's too much of a Sahib to run a fellow in forever and ever just because he got messed up with a bit of fluff."

They didn't talk much after that, but Father Smith thought over what the major had said. Perhaps the major was right. Perhaps God didn't take the genial sins too seriously. After all, malice was necessary for the commission of mortal sin, and the majority of men who drank to excess and ran wild with the girls were at bottom decent fellows. Lying, cheating, stealing, underpaying employees, money-grubbing, and mouthing big phrases to hide little thoughts—these were the sins that cried to God for punishment, since they harmed others more than their perpetrators. And yet being a decent fellow wasn't enough. The practice of a more heroic virtue was required if society as well as the individual was to be saved; but now that men had learned to be heroic in war, perhaps they would learn to be heroic in peace. Father Smith hoped that they would. The glow of the stars on the helmets of the marching men made them look very beautiful and austere. The crunch, crunch, crunch, of their feet beat the priest's hope into certainty. After all, they were brave men, and brave men could not possibly go back to the old cowardice. "Beatus vir qui timet Dominum," Father Smith murmured, and this time he found no difficulty in going on with the psalm.

X

THEY WERE TO attack at dawn three mornings later. Father Smith said Mass at three o'clock in the major's dugout. He wore the vestments that Mother de la Tour had embroidered for him. Cloth of gold on one side, because cloth of gold could be used on all feasts and ferial days, and black on the other, because there were always requiems to be said, with so many poor fellows being killed.

Most of the Catholics in the battalion came to Mass and Holy Communion. Father Smith heard their confessions first, because they hadn't all been as good as they should have been, what with the red wine in the estaminets and the girls and all that. As there were almost fifty of them, the priest had to start in quite early—at one-thirty, to be precise—which left only two minutes for each confession, so that mortal sins came spurting out at a fine rate and were as quickly polished off. The priest wanted to begin by hearing the boozy major's confession, but the major said that if Father Smith didn't mind, he'd very much rather bat last, because there was no saying how many more sins he could commit in ninety minutes. So Father Smith sat on his packing cases and heard the old, old tales of human frailty, and the major was last man in, and he wasn't so very original either, but perhaps that was because he had scarcely had much opportunity since his last confession three days previously: bless him, Father, for he had sinned, and last morning at stand-to he had been dreaming that he had been talking to a pretty girl in green silk pantaloons and a blighter of a sergeant major had woken him up, and when he had gone back to sleep, he had tried to dream about her again because she really was a corker, bless him, Father, with eyes that were blue one moment and violet the next.

The priest used the packing case he had been sitting on to hear confessions for his altar, with his portable altar stone and two candles and a crucifix. As he turned and saw in the blur of the candle-light the men's stern faces sweetly praying, he knew that this was how Mass should always be said, in a great hush and near death. There was no bell to ring at the Sanctus, so the major beat a tea-spoon against a tin mug, and it sounded quite holy. It sounded even holier at the Elevation, with Christ again in the Host and trembling in the shadows of the wine. Praying on above the mystery, Father Smith thanked the great, good God for this one safe, sure little miracle that He had promised would endure forever, that men might be drawn from their sins and fastened to the bright things of Heaven. Then he was down among them, giving them Communion, thrusting God under their roofs, that they might be cleansed from the great stinking abomination of the world and know Him again when He smiled at them in Paradise.

Too soon was the magic over and the world back again with stark immediate things to be done. As soon as he had unvested, Father Smith went out to make his thanksgiving among the cold piled sandbags. As he stood on the parapet praying out across the invisible grasses, the sky began to lighten, and the priest knew that it would soon be dawn. Slowly, the blue was draining from the sky, and the stars were going out, and the earth hardening out again flat and unmysterious from its crenellation of huddle and hill.

BRUCE MARSHALL

Father Smith looked at the sentry standing a few feet away from him and wondered if he was being afraid to die. Then, as the darkness lessened, the man's aspect grew familiar, and with a start the priest recognized Angus McNab.

"Angus, my boy, what on earth are you doing here?" the priest cried.

"Heavens, Father Smith!" the young man exclaimed. "I never kent that it was you was the R.C. padre. I only got back two days ago. Been back in Blighty for three months. Got a nice little packet in the airm. Nothing much really, just a flesh wound, but enough to keep me out of this sort of thing, thank God."

The young man's tone and bearing frightened the priest.

"Angus, what's come over you?" he asked. "Why were you not at confession and Holy Communion just now?"

"Och, Hell, Father, don't let's talk about religion if you don't mind," Angus said.

"My son, that's no way to speak to your old parish priest," Father Smith said sternly. "And we *are* going to talk about religion, because religion's the only thing that's really worth talking about, and you know that every bit as well as I do." He looked into the young man's eyes and away down the years, back to when the boy had been his acolyte and had freckles on his nose and sometimes a dirty smudge round his mouth. "Angus, Angus, who's been getting at you?" he asked.

"Nobody's been getting at me, Father," the young man said. "I just ken that religion's all havers, that's all. And the people at home are all havers too. They pretend to care an awful lot about what happens to us puir sods out here, but they don't really, not deep down in their hearts they dinna. They sing an awful lot about keeping the hame fires burning and loving you and kissing you when you come back again, but it's only words. All they want is to

89

stay at hame and be safe and have a good time. I ken because I've been on sick leave, and the folks didn't want to listen at all to what I had to tell them about things out here at the front. I ken because their eyes got empty and they were awa' off talking about something else before I'd finished speaking. And when I got on the tram with my sair airm in a great muckle splint and a yelly plaister, the auld bitches let on they didna see me but sat on their great muckle doups clavering away about the price of tea and Mary Pickford and me with ma puir sticking-oot airm getting in everybody's way and nearly being cowped every time the tram turned a corner like. And the young lassies were just as bad. Christians! yon's no Christians! And it's for the likes o' them that I'm expected to hae me belly blawn oot aboot ma heid and to die a sair, sair death." He suddenly clutched the priest. "Father, Father, make them stop it. Make them no make me go over again. Father, Father, I'm that feared."

The priest let the boy weep a little, because he knew that tears, if they flowed long enough, could float many a soul back to God.

"Angus, how old will you be now?" he asked at length.

"Twenty, Father," the boy answered.

"Twenty, Angus, and you think yourself wiser than all the saints and doctors of the Church. Shame on you, Angus. Now you just stand there and tell me all you've done since your last confession. No, you needn't kneel. Just look put across no-man's-land and be a sentry still, but get your sins quickly off your soul, because the battle'll soon be beginning and we've no time to lose."

When he had confessed Angus and given him absolution, the sky began to pale rapidly, but Father Smith still went on talking to the boy, because he still had some ghostly counsel to give.

"Listen, Angus," he said, "you mustn't be afraid to die, because you're in a state of grace now and ready to appear before our Lord.

And you mustn't worry too much about the people at home being thoughtless and not understanding about the war. It's just lack of imagination, that's all. They'll understand all right when peace comes and they'll see what kind of world we've won for them. For the world's going to be a very wonderful place after the war, Angus, much more the Kingdom of our Blessed Lord than ever it's been before."

"You're sure of that, Father?" The young man's eyes were shining now and not with tears.

"I'm sure of it, Angus. The bishop says so. Everybody says so. Besides, it's only common sense. Men aren't going back to being mean and petty and selfish after standing up for years and years to this sort of thing."

"What about the German and the Austrian Catholics, Father? Are they fighting for a better world too?"

"They've been misled by their temporal rulers in political matters, but once we've won our victory, the scales will fall from their eyes, and God's garment will be knit whole again," Father Smith said.

"I don't think I'd mind so much dying for that sort of world, Father," Angus said. "Thanks, Father, for helping me." He self-consciously shook hands with the priest. "I'm afraid I've been no end of a silly gowk," he said.

They couldn't talk at all after that, because the barrage began, and the men came streaming up into the trenches and stood crouching under the parapet in their steel helmets. Some of them were joking and some of them stood drawn into themselves and grave, but through all of them the same question ran: "Will it happen to *me*?" The noise of the guns and of the shells bursting was terrific. The priest wondered how the Germans were liking it and if they, too, were standing hammered into sanctity at the thought of the attack that they must know must be coming. He wondered, too, if there were Catholics among them and if a priest had just given them Holy Communion too, and how our Lord kept judging the Germans and the Britons that must forever be trooping before Him, red and angry from the battlefield. Then he was afraid for himself, for he knew that he, too, might die at any moment, and he wanted to go on living among advertisements for cigarettes and soot and chemist shops and sin, which was foolish of him, because the next world must be ever so much pleasanter.

Then an officer was beside him looking at his watch, and Father Smith made the sign of the cross and murmured the words of the general absolution, and even some of those who weren't Catholics bowed their heads because they knew that Father Smith was a priest and that he was praying for them. Then their bayonets pointed again, and their steel helmets were clamped down on their heads, and they were all priests and victims together and had never invited pretty girls to cricket matches or listened to water lapping under a rowing boat. Then somebody shouted and they were all gone, over and up and forward into the blast.

Father Smith didn't see Angus go over the top, but when he went forward with his holy oils, he came upon the boozy major lying wounded in a shell hole, with a great bloody gape in his belly.

"It's all right, Father; I still think God is a Sahib," he said as the priest bent to anoint him.

XI

FATHER SMITH HAD to be brave again on other occasions, but he didn't win the Victoria Cross or the Distinguished Service Order or the Military Cross, and so there was no deputation at the station to greet him when he came back from the war at the beginning of 1919, because everybody was coming back from the war these days. The bishop, however, was there, waiting on the platform bang in front of the bookstall, piled with *The Book of Artemas* and *The Young Visiters*, both of which were reputed to be very funny.

The bishop broke the bad news in the cab on the way to the presbytery.

"I am sending you back to the Holy Name, Father, but I am afraid that I shall have to allow Father Bonnyboat to remain on as rector," he said. "You see, you've been away for three years now, and so much has happened during your absence. The church has been completed, and a new set of Stations of the Cross blessed, and Lady Ippecacuanha received into the Church. I am sure that you will understand that when Father Bonnyboat has worked such wonders, it would be ungracious on my part to send him back to Our Lady, Mirror of Justice, especially when Father McGeechie is doing so well there himself. I know that this may sound harsh and even ungrateful, but I hope that you will understand that my decision has been prompted by the considerations of the good of the diocese as a whole."

Father Smith had to swallow hard before he was able to answer the bishop. He was fifty-one now, and it was he who had done the spade work on the Holy Name just as it was he who had done the spade work on Lady Ippecacuanha, and he thought that it was only fair that he should have had the parish for his own, with a curate to say the earlier Masses and take the more distant sick calls. Then he reminded himself of the vows he had made at his ordination and said humbly: "My lord, I am only too glad to be back at my old church in whatever capacity. You may rely on me to give the same allegiance to Father Bonnyboat as my rector as I have always given to your lordship as my bishop."

"Thank you, Father," the bishop said.

They talked of more general matters after that. The bishop said that although he still maintained that the war had been fought in defense of a righteous cause, he was disappointed to notice that as yet there was no sign of a religious awakening in the land. Indeed, the men returning from the army seemed to be restless and pleasure-seeking and were infecting their women folk with the same spirit. In industry, little or no attention was being paid to the maxims laid down by Pope Leo XIII in his encyclical *Rerum Novarum*, and employers were again seeking to increase their profits by paying scanty wages. In literature and on the stage and on the screen, the acquisition of wealth and the gratification of sexual passion were being represented as the only worthwhile objectives in life. In fashion, young women were shortening their hair and their skirts and behaving as immodestly as they dressed.

Father Smith said that he was sorry to have to state that he had remarked the same lack of religious fervor among people as a whole but hoped that the phenomenon was only temporary. After all, both his lordship and he must remember that the men had had a hard time of it in the trenches during the past four years and that it was perhaps natural that they should find it difficult to settle down, especially if, as the bishop said, civilian employers were unwilling to pay them decent wages. As for women's clothes, he had always felt that it was what women concealed and not what they revealed that did the harm, and that the best way to make men pure would be to let all the women in the country walk about naked, so that perhaps the shortening of their skirts was a step in the right direction. The bishop was rather silent when Father Smith said this, and the priest wondered if he had gone too far and led his lordship to think that life in the army had made him rather worldly. He hastened, therefore, to add that, like the bishop, he still hoped earnestly for a religious revival, because it was only in consciously seeking to serve our Lord that men could hope to find true peace.

Father Bonnyboat was standing in the doorway of the presbytery to greet them and said that, of course, the bishop would stay for supper; and the bishop said that it was really very nice of Father Bonnyboat but that he must hurry on back home because he still had a lot of his Office to say. Father Bonnyboat said that he quite understood, but Father Smith wondered if it was because of what he had said about women wearing no clothes that the bishop didn't want to stay to supper.

Father Smith thought that Father Bonnyboat had aged slightly since he had last seen him. His face seemed to have grown more leathery, and his hair was thinner, and behind his glasses his eyes were paler and colder. They did not talk much during supper, which consisted of tea and bread-and-butter and kippers. Father Bonnyboat asked Father Smith some questions about life in the army, but Father Smith could see that he wasn't really interested.

Father Smith didn't ask Father Bonnyboat any questions about the parish, because he thought that he still knew the parish better than Father Bonnyboat did and because he was still trying to get used to the idea of having him as a rector.

"I am afraid, Father, that you'll find that I have made some changes since you've been away," Father Bonnyboat said at length.

Father Smith was silent. He thought that he knew what was coming. Father Bonnyboat was a liturgical scholar and knew exactly how a Benedictine abbot should sing Pontifical High Mass on a double of the second class in the presence of a cardinal archbishop of the Ambrosian rite. He himself had never been great shakes at liturgy, although he had tried to be, because he knew that liturgy was only another name for Almighty God's table manners; but both his build and his voice had been against him, and he knew that there was all the difference in the world between a monk from Solesmes singing Mass and himself singing Mass, and he never could remember whether the Feast of the Holy Innocents was red or violet when it fell on a Sunday.

"I am referring to liturgical matters, of course," Father Bonnyboat went on. "To be quite frank, when I arrived here, I found things rather slack. I've scrapped the Roman vestments for Gothic, and I've also got rid of Miss O'Hara and her mixed choir."

Father Smith almost let out a howl.

"But how on earth's the poor woman going to earn her living?" he asked.

"They've taken her on at the pro-cathedral," Father Bonnyboat said. "Monsignor O'Duffy's not quite as particular in these matters as I am."

Father Smith wanted to cry out that Monsignor O'Duffy was quite right and that kindness to a good woman was more important than the sound of an introit or the set of a biretta; but instead he said:

"But she's been with me for more than ten years now."

"I am perfectly well aware of that. But you know the motto, 'Nihil operi Dei praeponatur'; let nothing be put before God's office."

"I also know a text . . ." Father Smith wanted to say, but instead he marched over to the window and looked out. At first he didn't see the cinema, because he was trying to pray for Father Bonnyboat and was finding it very difficult. When he did see the cinema, he noticed that it was all lighted up in red and purple and gold and with new names plastered across it: Constance Talmadge, Norma Talmadge, Thomas Meighan. The old notice about afternoon tea being served free of charge to patrons seemed to have gone, and the prices of admission were now a shilling for adults and sixpence for children, but the queue of people waiting for admission seemed longer than ever. Beside the queue, a man wearing an officer's British warm was turning the handle of a hurdy-gurdy, but people were looking away haughtily when he approached with his hat. On the steps of the cinema itself stood Angus McNab in dark green commissionaire's uniform with the blue-and-red ribbon of the Distinguished Conduct Medal on his breast. Father Smith was glad to see that Angus had found a job, even if the ex-officer hadn't, but it was of the ex-officer that he was thinking when he turned again to face Father Bonnyboat.

"Perhaps there's something that God thinks even more important than liturgy, Father," he said. "I mean justice and decency and human kindness. And that's precisely what those who have fought and risked all for us don't seem to be getting."

To his surprise, Father Bonnyboat didn't bark back at him but came over and stood with him at the window and took his arm.

"You're right and you're wrong, Father," he said. "You're right because man can't live by liturgy alone, and you're wrong because man needs beauty in his soul as well as bread in his belly. Tell me: what do you think all these people are standing out there in that queue for if it isn't to slake their longing for excitement and romance and beauty? And Almighty God is ever so much more exciting and romantic and beautiful than the heroine of any cinematograph film, only people don't know that. It's up to us priests of the Catholic Church to make them see it, and that's why we are right to make our services as lovely and austere as possible, because like that we're not only honoring God ourselves but we're making other people honor Him too. And when they honor Him, they can't help being more kindly and charitable to their fellow men, who also are made in His image. I know, Father, that you're impatient to see the good come out of this horrible war we've just been fighting, but believe me, God's old, slow, sure way of calling men is still the best."

Father Smith was smiling as he allowed himself to be led back to the table, because he knew that it wasn't going to be difficult any longer for him to pray for Father Bonnyboat, because Father Bonnyboat was as eager as himself about the Lord's cause, only in a different way, that was all.

XII

ON THE FEAST of Saint Andrew, 1919, when Father Smith went as usual to say his prayers in the High Kirk, there were still no signs of a religious revival in the land, although there was plenty of culture flying about: a new novel by Hugh Walpole, and *Abraham Lincoln* by John Drinkwater at the Lyric Hammersmith, and of course, Germany Was Going to Pay, and the railway strike had been settled satisfactorily, and Miss Lee White was singing husky little songs in revue, and there were plenty of fat jobs going at Geneva, and young men passed by their window and oh, they sang softly, so softly, their dear, but all that didn't seem to mean that the Lord was coming again in power and great glory or, what Father Smith thought even more important, that people were creeping back humbly and contritely to the Lord. So when he had prayed for Scotland, that God might give her back the light that she had lost, Father Smith prayed for the world as well and for its rulers, and for Arnold Bennett, H. G. Wells, and Horatio Bottomley, that God might give them wisdom and understanding when they wrote articles for the press.

The minister was standing again under his high hat on the porch when Father Smith came out. They greeted one another affably and, when they had spoken of the weather, the new work-men's model cottages, and Mr. Bonar Law, Father Smith asked the minister point-blank if he had noticed any stirrings of spiritual awakening in his congregation.

"I'm afraid not, Father," the minister answered. "Like you, I was hoping for great things, but it seems that they are just not to be."

"I wonder if it is because people have lived too much in crowds these last few years," Father Smith said. "I have often noticed that the intelligence of any gathering of people is always in inverse ratio to the numbers present. Perhaps it is the same with piety. Perhaps our Lord intended that we should interpret Him literally when He said, 'When two or three are gathered together in My Name, lo, there am I in the midst of them.' Perhaps He meant that when six or seven were gathered together, even in His Name, He would be less in the midst of them. In any case, it is certain that when great crowds of people are gathered together, He is not in the midst of them, or if He is, the crowd pay no attention to Him."

"But that is when they are not gathered together in His Name," the minister said.

"If we are really Christians, there should be no occasion on which we are not gathered together in His Name," the priest said. "He should be in our ballrooms and theaters just as He is in our churches. But we are afraid to be ourselves in crowds, because we are afraid not to be like what we think our neighbors are, and our neighbors are afraid not to be like what they think we are. And so everybody pretends to be less pious, less virtuous, less honorable than he really is."

"I think, with your permission, that I shall use that in a sermon sometime," the minister said.

"It's what I call the new hypocrisy," Father Smith said. "In the old days, people pretended to be better than they were, but now they pretend to be worse. In the old days, a man said that he went to church on Sundays even if he didn't, but now he says he plays golf and would be very distressed if his men friends found out that he really went to church. In other words, hypocrisy used to be what a French writer calls the tribute vice paid to virtue, but now it's the tribute virtue pays to vice; and that, I think, is a very much worse state of affairs, because it means that our standards have declined and that we no longer dare to be private, honest people but are instead becoming inside the façades we pretend, out of motives of human respect, to be outside."

The minister did not answer, but Father Smith could see that he was thinking a lot. In front of them, two young girls stood on the top of the steps with their short skirts blowing across the trees on the edge of Sir Dugald Ippecacuanha's estate.

"Of course, Jim can't stand that sort of thing at all," one of them said. "He's terribly you know what I mean."

"I know, Alec's like that too," the second girl said.

"Funny, isn't it?" the first girl said.

"Of course, it does make a difference when you use fish knives," the second girl said.

They stood for a minute or two, mooning out over the city. Under their transparent blouses, the trigonometry of their straps, strings, and tapes crossed and recrossed like railway lines at Crewe.

"Well, cheerio," the first girl said.

"Cheerio, then," the second girl said.

They walked away down different sides of the steps, their wiggling little bottoms wiser than Aristotle.

"Did you hear that?" Father Smith said. "They're frightened to say 'goodbye' because it means something; they say 'cheerio,' which, apart from being the ugliest word I know, means and is intended to mean absolutely nothing. Soon they won't be able to *feel* 'goodbye' or 'good health' or any other decent human sentiment."

"They're modern, I suppose," the minister said.

"Pagan, you mean," the priest said, and then laughed aloud, in case the minister should think that he was altogether too upstagy in his likes and dislikes.

XIII

WHEN ON ASH Wednesday, 1920, there were still no signs of a religious revival in the land, even Father Bonnyboat began to be afraid that liturgy alone wouldn't do the trick, so he asked Monsignor O'Duffy to come along from the pro-cathedral and preach a mission. Monsignor O'Duffy said that he thought that a grand idea and that he would preach the congregation of the Holy Name such a humdinger of a mission that nobody in the whole parish would commit a mortal sin for three weeks at least, only he thought the sooner he got going the better, because the devil was out with a blare and blast these days and no mistake. So the mission started on the first Sunday in Lent, with High Mass by Monsignor O'Duffy himself. He preached his first sermon from the altar steps and after the priest's Communion instead of after the Gospel, because he had made up his mind to preach a snorter of a sermon and didn't want to have to do a lot of high-class singing afterward.

"Stand away from yon door," he bawled down the church at the pass-keepers, "stand away from yon door so that I can see if anybody tries for to get out. Move up there and let the lassie in," he bellowed at Lady Ippecacuanha. "Ye canna have the corner seat all the time. In the Name of the Father, and of the Son, and of the

Holy Ghost. Amen. My dear brethren, as there is so much sin rampant in this parish, your good rector has called me in to give a mission and to frighten you back into the way of the Lord. As a matter of fact, I propose to give two missions: one in the English language for Scots and Irish people and one in the Eyetalian language for Eyetalian people. The Scots and Irish mission will be at eight o'clock in the evenings, and the Eyetalian mission will be at seven o'clock in the evenings, but let me point out that it's no good one Eyetalian from each family attending the Eyetalian mission, but every Eyetalian in the parish must attend.

"My dear brethren in Jesus Christ, looking out upon the world today we see a great roaring, grunting, boozing, lusting, blaspheming, ranting, rampaging heathen mass swarming along the pavements of our cities and thinking themselves respectable citizens just because they wear hats on their heids and mackintoshes you can see through and carry umberellies forbye. But they're no respectable. They're no respectable because they pay no attention to God's Commandments. And this great roaring, grunting, boozing, lusting, blaspheming, ranting, rampaging heathen mass will gang doon the drain tae burn in Hell fire for all eternity if it's no very careful. And you, my dear brethren in Jesus Christ, are part of this great roaring, grunting, boozing, lusting, blaspheming, ranting, rampaging heathen mass."

Father Smith, who was subdeacon, gave up listening at this point, although from time to time he caught one of the monsignor's phrases, cracking across the church with a fine smack: "No young couples in this parish should walk down dark lanes after ten o'clock at night"; "Almighty God never intended young girls to wear flesh-colored silk stockings at any time of the year, let alone during the holy season of Lent." Was this, after all, what was wanted? Was it not an awakening to the more subtle requirements of the Lord's service that was needed? The gaudy sins had to be avoided, of course, because drunkenness and fornication clouded the lens of the soul and hid the cool vision of God from those who committed them. But was not respectability, which banned drunkenness and fornication almost as rigorously as did the Church of God, was not respectability the greatest sin of all, since it mistook semblance for sincerity? The bank managers, the stockbrokers, the lawyers, the company directors, those who encouraged young men to get on in the world and lose the glow in their eyes, were not they bigger sinners than the drunkards and the fornicators, since the sins they committed in their counting-houses spread out all over the world and stained the innocent? But there were no bank managers, stockbrokers, lawyers, or company directors in the congregation of the Holy Name, because in Scotland, only the poor were Catholics. Perhaps that was why God loved them so much and gave them only the easier hoops to jump through, sobriety and purity, because they had had such a rough lot on earth that it was only fair that they should be allowed into Heaven more easily than the rich. He glanced along the sedilia to see how Father Bonnyboat was taking the sermon, but Father Bonnyboat was sitting with his biretta cocked well over his eyes so that it was impossible to tell what he was thinking.

At the top of the altar steps, after having warned those who had never been further afield than Dunoon about the dangers to be met in Paris from "bedizened and bejeweled Jezebels, flaunting their baseness in marble palaces," Monsignor O'Duffy drew thunderingly to a close. "Aye and I ken fine what you're thinking," he said. "Ye're thinking that och that's all very well and that you've plenty of time for repentance before ye die and that ye might as well have another wee keek at the world, the flesh, and the devil, and maybe another wee taste as well. Well, you've no got plenty of time. This very night the Lord may say to any of you, 'Aundry or Bessie or Jimmie, thy soul is required of thee,' and if it's no free from mortal sin and as bricht as a polished frying pan in a well-kept kitchen doon, ye'll gang to Hell to yell and shriek for all eternity with the damned. Twenty years ago, in this very town, there were two miners: one was called Pat and the other was called Mike, and neither of them had been to their Easter duties for years. And one fine day, I met them both in the street and I said to them, 'Pat and Mike,' I said, 'Pat and Mike, ye both ken just as well as I do what'll happen to you if you die without going to confession and Holy Communion.' Well, Pat listened to my warning and went to his duties, but Mike didn't listen, and the next time I saw Mike there, he was on the floor, vomiting oot his heart's blood. A blessing that I wish you all in the Name of the Father, and of the Son, and of the Holy Ghost. Amen."

Exceptionally, Benediction of the Blessed Sacrament was given after Mass, because it was a special occasion. As Father Smith knelt in front of the Host in the monstrance, he thanked Almighty God again for having given the Church hard, certain words that could not fail however much priests might flop and flounder in the pulpit when they spoke with their own human voices. The new male choir in their starched surplices sang the *O Salutaris* and the *Tantum Ergo* with happy vehemence, but Father Smith did not think they sang it any more beautifully than Miss O'Hara's cock-and-hen choir with their gaiters, their goloshes, and their false notes. Then Monsignor O'Duffy raised the monstrance and made with it a big sign of the cross over all the kneeling people, and Father Smith could see that his big, sweating face was really loving our Lord and that shouting and ranting and fuming was just his way of trying to make other people love Him too.

As he passed down the church after the service, Father Smith saw quite a crowd of women lined up on a bench outside the confessional that had been allocated to Monsignor O'Duffy for the duration of the mission. Lady Ippecacuanha was among them, and there was a slattern or two, for the monsignor had quite a way with the ladies of the profession when they accosted him in error at night when he was returning from sick calls. "Ye'll burn like kindling, you scum," he would roar, instead of taking off his hat like the Episcopal dean and saying, "Not tonight, my dear." Even now he was lecturing them prior to entering his confessional, standing in front of them and shouting out his injunctions at the feather in Lady Ippecacuanha's hat. "I'm delighted to see that my words have had such good effect, but please cut out the havers when you make your confessions because I'm in a hurry to get home for my dinner," he was saying. "So begin at once with your real sins, such as when you were last drunk and all that, and remember that it's no use confessing that you stole a rope if you forget to mention that there was a horse tied to the other end of it."

At the back of the church, where the very poor worshipped, there was the usual smell of dirty clothes and human sweat, but Father Smith didn't mind it too much, because he knew that it was the odor of sanctity, although he hoped that God would give the poor a more pleasant perfume in Paradise. Each time he smelled that smell, he knew what Christ had meant when He had said, "For the first shall be last and the last shall be first," and it pleased him to think that one day the poor would have compensation for all their discomforts and humiliations, when they sat back in the front row of the stalls in high Heaven and cried cock-a-hoop to God with Saint Ignatius and Saint Dominic and all the rest of the aristocracy.

At the back of the church, among the piles of tracts and the ropes of rosaries and the platoons of Sacred Hearts, he came upon

Angus McNab and Annie Rooney standing arm-in-arm. He smiled at Angus McNab because he had been so brave and won the D.C.M., but he did not smile at Annie Rooney, because he knew that it was still years and years since she had last been to the Sacraments. Angus was wearing a new brown suit that seemed all curves and smart creases, but Father Smith thought that he didn't look half as smart as he did in his commissionaire's uniform, parading up and down outside the advertisements for Mae Murray and Eddie Lyons and Lee Moran. Annie Rooney was dressed in the height of fashion too, in a pale blue costume and a pink blouse so low cut that it had only one button on it.

"Father, you'll have to congratulate us," Angus said. "Annie and me's getting married."

The news was a blow to Father Smith, because he had always liked Angus and he knew that Annie Rooney was just a baggage, tarting it round with drunken sailors whenever she had the chance; but he couldn't say that to Angus McNab now, not with Annie Rooney standing there staring at him out of her great hostile cat's eyes.

"Marriage is a sacrament of the Church and not to be entered upon lightly," he said, more to Annie Rooney than to Angus, but for all the effect the remark made on her great puffed-out face, he saw that he might just as well have said: "As the Church teaches that the moon is made of green cheese, no Catholic has the right to believe that it is made of butter."

"It's all right, Father," Angus said. "Annie's a good girl now, and we're both coming to Holy Communion together before we're married, aren't we, Annie?"

Annie neither answered nor smiled but nodded her head several times at Father Smith to make the priest realize that things were all right really and that deep down beneath her pink blouse

Annie was a true Christian, although she didn't take much pains to let people know.

Monsignor O'Duffy was still hearing confessions when Father Smith turned back into the church, but the mutter of his voice came quite quietly from the box, as though even he knew that a priest had to be tender and soothing when applying the merits of Christ's Passion to weak human souls.

XIV

IN JULY, 1922, there were now so many pupils at the nuns' school that Reverend Mother felt quite justified in asking Lady Ippecacuanha to present the prizes, and Lady Ippecacuanha was graciously pleased to accept, appearing on the platform in a new check costume with a copy of *If Winter Comes* under one arm and a roll of music under the other, because there was to be a concert afterward and she had also been invited to sing. Her Greek god of a son came too, only he was no longer a Greek god, because he had been so hacked about in the war, but he looked so saintly on his crutches that the nuns all felt sure that he would become a Catholic, too, one of these fine days. His lordship the bishop was also on the platform, on the right of Reverend Mother, with the sun making him blink behind his glasses, and Mother Leclerc and Mother de la Tour were on the platform as well, because they were the most important nuns after Reverend Mother. Monsignor O'Duffy was among the grand persons too, sitting in the second row to hide his big feet, so he said, and wearing the new purple stock that he had bought in Rome the year before when he had had a fine pow-wow with the pope. Father Bonnyboat and Father Smith were there as well, only Father Bonnyboat now signed himself Christopher Canon Bonnyboat because he had been promoted by the bishop.

The proceedings opened with prayer by the bishop and a little speech by the bishop, in which his lordship said that Catholic youth would do well to turn its eyes to Italy, where a man called Mussolini was doing so much for his country, and Lady Ippecacuanha clapped and said, "Hear, hear," because she knew Italy well, having once lost her connection at Ventimiglia.

Then Lady Ippecacuanha stood up to present the prizes and said how very proud she was to do so. While congratulating those who had won prizes, she reminded those who had not that it was not always the girl who won the most prizes at the school who got on best in life. However, she hoped that they would all go on working hard and trying to please the nuns, who were imparting to them both knowledge and character so that they might grow up fine and worthy women. And women in the new world were going to have ever such a better chance than women in the old world, because the war to end wars had been fought and won, and now they would be able to become worthy mothers of tomorrow. Father Smith looked along at the bishop to see how he was taking this part of Lady Ippecacuanha's speech, but his lordship's face was wreathed in a smile of benign approval, so the priest concluded that the war must have been properly won, after all, although the people as a whole didn't seem any more religious than they had been in the past and the nuns hadn't been allowed back to France and there had been a big coal strike only the previous year.

The children, however, looked very sweet as they went up to get their prizes, curtseying to the bishop and Reverend Mother and Lady Ippecacuanha, who dished out the works of Miss Bessie Marchant with brisk benevolence. Elvira Sarno received three prizes: one for elocution, one for Christian doctrine, and one for French. She was fourteen now and very dark and grave and lovely in her white dress, and everybody clapped a lot when she received her prizes. When she came up for the third time, Reverend Mother leaned forward and seemed to whisper something quite special to the bishop, and his lordship nodded his wise old head several times and looked very pleased.

The concert followed immediately afterward, and the nuns and the clergy all got down from the platform to make room for the performers, with the exception of Monsignor O'Duffy, who was to play the accompaniments. Lady Ippecacuanha opened the concert by singing "Down in the Forest Something Stirred." She had wanted to sing her old favorite "Have You Ever Seen an Oyster Walk Upstairs?" but her husband had suggested that it would perhaps sound rather horsey in a convent, old gal, and that she had better choose something more poetic, but with nothing about spooning by the light of the silvery moon in it, because the nuns probably wouldn't like that either. She was hugely applauded and was about to sing "I'll Sing Thee Songs of Araby" as an encore, but Reverend Mother came forward and explained that, much as they had enjoyed her ladyship's singing, there really wasn't time. Then Canon Bonnyboat sang Mozart's "Ave Verum Corpus," which made everybody feel quite religious, because he was a very fine singer and meant every word he sang. After that, Elvira Sarno recited King Henry V's speech before the battle of Agincourt with such verve that she brought the house down. As the clear, young voice said out the thrilling words, deep down within him, Father Smith wondered if it wasn't wrong to teach children to recite poems about war, however beautifully they were written, but he supposed that he must be wrong, otherwise the clergy and the nuns would not have applauded so loudly; and anyway, if one went as far as that, there were quite a lot of other customs in the world one would have to change, such as giving small boys toy soldiers at Christmas, for example. Then Monsignor O'Duffy rose and said that, by the shamrock, everybody was getting applauded except the priest at the piany, and that whether they wanted it or not, he was bally well going to sing them "Danny Boy," and sing them "Danny Boy" he did, and Lady Ippecacuanha whispered to the bishop that she really thought it rather sporting of the monsignor to have used a great, big, manly word like "bally."

Tea was served in the refectory, with the bishop and Reverend Mother and the clergy all sitting at a special table with plenty of penny pink iced cakes, only now they cost two pence because of the war. The bishop said that he very much disapproved of a new game that the university students had started recently, that of shouting out "beaver" at the top of their voices whenever they met in the street a man with a beard, and he believed that there was something even ruder that they shouted when they met a man with a beard riding a green bicycle, which, fortunately, wasn't often. The custom was doubly deplorable from the point of view of Catholics, because not only was it a breach of good manners, which was another name for charity, which was another name for doing unto others as you would they should do unto you, but it was also highly discourteous to missionaries, and it appeared that the poor Franciscan friars at Kincairns had been having a pretty poor time of late. With his mouth bung full of two-penny cake, Monsignor O'Duffy said that that just showed ye that the youth of the country was in the toils of the Jews, the Sunday press, and Satan, but Reverend Mother said she didn't think the offense quite as serious as all that, and that no doubt the craze would soon pass and that the friars at Kincairns would be well advised to apply the merit they gained from their discomfort to the suffering souls in Purgatory.

The grass smelled soft and fresh and green when they all went out on the lawn for the sports afterward. Mother de la Tour said that they must be careful not to spoil the flowers, because they were the Lord's handiwork. Monsignor O'Duffy was the official starter, and he fairly enjoyed firing the pistol, screwing up his eyes and holding his great ham of a hand high in the air. Watching the happy pattern of the girls running and the nuns' habits beside the trees and Mother Leclerc fishing for her spectacles in her huge, wide pocket, Father Smith breathed a swift prayer of thanks to God for having made holiness so simple and so joyful and so beautiful. Blinking the glad tears back from his eyes, he saw Elvira Sarno standing in front of him with Joseph Scott, who was now at Saint Francis Xavier's Academy but had been invited across for the afternoon.

"Father, Jo and I have just been having a terrible argument," she announced.

"Elvira says that it's a sin to drink lemonade when you're in retreat and I say it isn't," the boy said.

Bless them, bless them, Father Smith thought, and he was about to explain that there was no real theological issue at stake unless one wanted to please our Lord by giving up something that one really liked when Elvira shouted out that there was the parents' race starting and that it looked as though Monsignor O'Duffy was going to run in it himself because he was handing over his pistol to the bishop. And run in the parents' race the monsignor did and came in puffing and blowing third last, even though he took off his frock coat and showed his licorice allsort shirtsleeves; but Elvira said to Joseph that they mustn't laugh at his shirts because her mother had told her that the monsignor always bought cheap shirts so that he might have more money to give away to the poor.

When the bishop had presented the prizes, Reverend Mother asked the clergy if they would be kind enough to come and see what was the matter with Mother de la Tour's wireless set, as the crystal didn't seem to be working properly and men knew so much more about these things than women. The bishop said that he knew nothing at all about these newfangled matters, but Monsignor O'Duffy said that he hadn't a brother who kept a wee bicycle shop in Inveraray for nothing. So they all trooped into the parlor, and Monsignor O'Duffy put on the earphones and scratched about the crystal right under the portrait of Pope Pius XI, who had so recently been elected to the Supreme Pontificate, and Mother de la Tour said, "C'était vraiment malheureux, mais elle n'y comprenait rien, mais absolument rien du tout." At first Monsignor O'Duffy said that he could hear nothing. Father Smith felt that it was a pity that one ever heard anything at all on wireless sets, because it seemed to him that new inventions were coming out much too quickly, and that if amusements went on becoming more and more mechanized as they seemed to be doing, people would no longer require to use their intelligence to fill their leisure, and literature, poetry, and drama would be pop goes the weasel *per omnia saecula saeculorum*; but he didn't say so, because he felt that it was up to the bishop. However, when Monsignor O'Duffy said that he thought he could hear a girl singing that "the roses round the door made her love mother more," he could contain himself no longer and said almost angrily that it was a pity that the fine inventions of scientific brains should be used for such mean ends and that it advanced people neither spiritually nor culturally that they should be able to hear from Scotland a girl in London debasing family life by singing sugary twaddle about mother-love.

Both the clergy and the nuns seemed so surprised by his vehemence that Father Smith hastened to add that he hadn't meant to criticize the nuns for having a wireless set. Reverend Mother said that that was quite all right and that she thought she understood what Father Smith meant. The bishop said he thought he understood too, but Monsignor O'Duffy said that all yon blether about culture was much too highfalutin' for him.

Walking back to the presbytery with Canon Bonnyboat, Father Smith thought that he saw Annie Rooney going into a bar with a sailor, but he told himself later that he must have made a mistake, for Annie Rooney had been married to Angus McNab for two years now and always brought her new hat to Mass on Sundays.

XV

FATHER SMITH FOUND it easy enough to pray for pagan peoples whom he had never seen, but there were still occasions on which he found it difficult to pray for Canon Bonnyboat, especially when the latter said the seven-o'clock Mass and got into breakfast before he did and bagged first shot at the *Highland Herald*. This afternoon, too, he was finding it difficult to pray for his rector, because the canon had just handed over to him for instruction a Protestant railway porter who wanted to marry a Catholic scullery-maid. For more than half an hour Father Smith had explained to the young man's big ears the doctrine of transubstantiation and how wonderful it was that our Lord should choose to remain on among us in this way, and then, when at the end of the lesson he had asked his catechumen Who was present in the Mass, the young man had replied: "I ken that one all right, Father; the Virgin Mary, of course."

He was just recovering from the shock when Brigid, the new housekeeper, announced that Elvira and Joseph were wanting to see him in the parlor.

"Buon giorno, carissimo padre mio," Elvira greeted, who often spoke to him in Italian now that she knew that Father Smith had studied in Rome. "E come sta?"

"Sto bene, grazie," the priest replied, loving the marvel of her accent, as true in Italian as in Scots. "E tu, come stai?"

"Benissimo," Elvira said, and added "per Bacco," because she knew the exclamation always amused the priest. "Joseph—no, shut up, Joseph, and let me do the talking—Joseph thinks that he would like to become a priest when he grows up, and he wants to know if you think he's holy enough."

"Per Bacco!" the priest exclaimed and laughed aloud for sheer joy, because it was all so heartening after what that dreadful young man had said about the Blessed Virgin being really and truly present in the Eucharist.

"You see, Father," the boy said gravely, "I want to do some good in the world, and I don't think I could ever be satisfied just going into business and making money."

"Laus Tibi, Christe," the priest sang silently in his heart; "praise be to Thee, O Christ, because Thou raisest up ever more priests and more poets to rhyme Thy honor and glory." He had always loved Joseph Scott since the day when, as a boy of four, he had come running up to him in the street and thrust his small hand into his and asked, "Can I chum you, Father?"

"How old are you now, Joseph?" he asked.

"Fifteen, Father," the boy answered.

"Well, you've got time enough to think it over, haven't you?" the priest said. "Remember that a priest's is a hard and difficult calling and is not to be entered upon lightly. But I am sure that if you still have the same dispositions in two or three years' time, you will make a very good priest indeed. And you, Elvira," he asked, because he felt that if he didn't make a joke he would disgrace himself by bursting out into tears, "you're not thinking of becoming a nun by any chance?"

Elvira shook her head smilingly.

"Not unless I could wear pretty dresses occasionally," she said. "Tell me, Father: do nuns *never* get into mufti?"

"Nuns never get into mufti because their souls never get into mufti," Father Smith said.

"It's not that I don't love our Lord, but I love pretty clothes as well," Elvira said. "Indeed, I rather think I want to become an actress and have the men all turn and stare at me when I walk into the lounge of the Carlton-Elite Hotel. Tell me, Father; is that very wicked of me?"

"She's terribly worldly, isn't she?" Joseph said.

"I know a lady who was told by a Jesuit that it might be her vocation to be the best-dressed woman in every room she walked into as long as she did it to the greater glory of God, so boo!" Elvira said.

"Most things are all right as long as we do them to the greater glory of God," Father Smith said. Then, feeling that perhaps he had been a little too sententious, he added: "You two seem great friends, don't you?"

"Perhaps that's because you baptized us both on the same day," Elvira said. They stood swinging hands in front of him quite naturally. "Tell us: did we cry much?"

"Do you know, I can't for the life of me remember," Father Smith said. "You see, I baptize so many babies."

"That's what must be so wonderful about a priest's life," Joseph said. "All the good that one's constantly doing."

"All God's beginnings and middlings and endings," Father Smith said. "It teaches you that a thousand years in God's sight are but an evening gone."

"Then you really think, Father, that I have got a vocation?" Joseph asked.

"I didn't say that yet, did I?" Father Smith laughed.

They went as they had come, hand-in-hand. Father Smith wondered for a moment if it was right for a boy who thought he had a vocation to the priesthood to be holding the hand of a girl so pretty as Elvira, but he told himself that they were both too young and innocent to realize that there could be any danger in their affection, and that our Lord Himself had said that unless people became as little children they should not enter the Kingdom of Heaven. Through the window, the advertisements for the cinema on the other side of the road were all about a lady called Nazimova, but the priest hadn't long to think about that because the presbytery bell rang again, and Brigid announced that Angus McNab was waiting to see him in the parlor.

Father Smith saw at once that something was wrong. The young man was untidy and disheveled and had an angry look burning in his eye.

"What for did you tell me wrong, Father?" he began at once. "What for did you tell me wrong?"

The priest said gently that he was afraid that he did not understand.

"Fine ye understand, and if ye dinna I'll tell ye," Angus ranted on. "Do you mean to say that ye dinna mind telling me in the trenches that people wouldn't be thoughtless anymore about the war, once it was over and won? 'The world's going to be a very wonderful place after the war, Angus,' ye said. Those were your very words, Father. I ken fine they were, because they've been aye dinging away in my ears ever since. Well, let me tell you that it's no wonderful at all. It's just a great, big, stinking, clarty pig's breakfast like it aye was. Distinguished Conduct Medal, indeed! Folk don't care aboot that sort of thing any mair. 'The war's over and done with now,' they say, 'and it's time you young lads settled down and forgot all yon blether aboot the trenches.' Aye, but *they* weren't in the trenches; *they* didna see the blood and the muck and the sclutter; they didna feel the sair bullets and steel in their bellies, so it's gey fine ham for them to talk. And *they* havna got to go tramping up and doon in front off a picture hoose and a lot of photies of rich lassies sliding their sleekit wee bodies in and oot of motor cars, and all for forty bob a week. And they dinna get the sack from a great, big, yellow dago when they get married and ask for a ten-bob rise and have their ain wee wife say that she canna go on living with them unless they make mair money and look slippy about it." His anger left him and he stood blubbering and snottering and twisting his hands. "Faither, I'm that miserable," he said.

Slowly, Father Smith drew the whole story from him. Soon after they had been married, Annie had told him that she couldn't possibly make both ends meet on two pounds a week. Whereupon Angus had gone to Signor Sarno and asked for an increase in wages, but Signor Sarno had said that forty shillings a week was all that he could afford to pay a commissionaire and that Angus could either take it or leave it. Angus had neither taken it nor left it but had tried to organize a strike among the employees of the cinema, and Signor Sarno had got to hear of it and had dismissed him. Since then, Angus had hunted in vain for employment, and Annie had threatened on more than one occasion to leave him.

As he prepared to deliver a little lecture on the mystery of suffering and the spiritual benefits to be derived from sorrow, Father Smith wondered if it had indeed been Annie whom he had seen with that sailor a year previously. Then he wondered what benefit he himself would have derived from a lecture on the mystery of suffering if he had had to live hard as Angus lived hard and had lost his job and had a floozy of a wife he couldn't trust out of his sight, so he changed his tactic and said that he would call personally on Signor Sarno and see if he couldn't prevail upon him to take Angus back.

"Thank you, Father," Angus said, wringing both the priest's hands. "And I'm sorry for what I said about you being wrang yon day in the trenches, because it's the world that's wrang and no you."

But Signor Sarno was quite adamant when Father Smith saw him half an hour later beneath a signed photograph of Pauline Frederick.

"Per Bacco, reverendo Father, but what you ask is impossible," he said. "A communista, that's what young McNab is. Seeking to ruin my business by inciting others to strike. Santa Madonna, that shall I not have. I do not like communistas, and I shall not employ them. And they are against our holy religion as His Holiness the pope has himself said and Monsignor O'Duffy has said too, on the Feast of the Immaculate Exception. And Mussolini, the leader of my so beautiful country, has said so too, per Bacco. Che puzza di merda, tutti quei communisti, excusing me for the rude word, reverendo Father. But Mussolini, he will chase them all out and my country shall be great again, so, oh so, so great, as you will see, reverendo Father."

"It is not countries that we want to be great but individual men," Father Smith said gently. "Great as our Lord would have them be great, not with trumpets and banners and guns and battleships, but in generosity, selflessness, and humility. And you, Signor Sarno, you would be very great indeed if you were to take Angus McNab back into your employment. I think that I can promise you that he will not be so foolish again. And he fought very valiantly indeed in the war, remember."

"So did millions of other young men, but they cannot expect to be heroes forever," Signor Sarno said. "And discipline is no less a heroism than facing bullets, as that great leader of my country, Benito Mussolini, has said, and one cannot maintain discipline unless one punishes those who offend against it. No, reverendo

Father, I regret exceedingly, but I shall be unable to do what you ask me. I am sorry for Angus McNab, but if he wants employment, he will require to look for it elsewhere."

When Father Smith came out of the cinema, they were taking down the advertisement about Nazimova and putting one up about a dog called Rin-Tin-Tin instead, because next day was Thursday when the program changed; but the priest did not notice, because he was too busy praying that Angus would find another job.

XVI

ON THE FEAST of Saint Andrew, 1924, when Father Smith went to say his prayers in the High Kirk, Angus still hadn't found a regular job and was making a living as best he could touting bootlaces and matches in the street and selling pencils from office to office. Of course, his red-and-blue D.C.M. ribbon helped a little, but not as much as it should, because businessmen were now saying that Britain had made only one mistake in the war and that was in fighting on the wrong side, and that in any case it hadn't been such a bad war for the soldiers as some of them tried to make out. There was no sign of a religious revival in the land either, but the clergy of all denominations didn't seem to be worrying about that any longer but instead were denouncing war as a crime, a treachery, and a cowardice, so perhaps it had been illogical to expect any good to come from it.

In the West End of London, Edna Best and Miss Tallulah Bankhead were most modern when they got tight, blotto, and squiffed together in *Fallen Angels*, a play by a young man called Noel Coward, who also had another two plays running simultaneously and was an actor himself as well and could play the piano quite dandy too. An older man called George Bernard Shaw also had a play called *Saint Joan* running, and there was a marvelous speech in it about the danger of heresy, but people who really knew were beginning to whisper that he wasn't a patch on Mr. Aldous Huxley's pants, which were very enlightened indeed. *The Constant Nymph* kept Mr. Augustine Birrell awake into the small hours of the morning, and *The Green Hats* grew all around. In politics, Mr. Ramsay MacDonald had come into power, but Signor Sarno still changed the advertisements outside his cinema twice a week, only the ladies that were appearing in the epoch-making, smashing slices of life were now called Miss Gloria Swanson and Miss Lillian Gish and Miss Pola Negri, and the great big world kept churning out Mr. William Gerhardi and Mr. Beverley Nichols, because there was room for them as well, and one was getting rather tired of Chesterton and Belloc and Wells and Galsworthy, although even stockbrokers knew that their works were literature, because they disliked reading them so much.

This year, when Father Smith came out from saying his prayers in the church, he didn't find the minister standing on the porch, but he found instead a painted golden young lady in a blue pleated frock. She regarded him with interest as he approached and asked him, with her frock blowing all about her lovely legs:

"Tell me," she asked, "do you get much response to the old, old story these days? I'm not asking out of idle curiosity but from professional interest. I'm a novelist, you see, and I have my public to satisfy."

"Well, Miss ..." the priest began.

"Miss Dana Agdala, author of *Naked and Unashamed*, twelve thousand copies here and twenty thousand in America, but perhaps you haven't read me."

"Well, Miss Agdala, if by 'response to the old, old story' you mean correspondence with sanctifying grace, I should say that the world is neither better nor worse than it was," Father Smith said. "You see, I'm a Catholic priest ..."

Miss Agdala regarded him with open-mouthed delight.

"A Catholic priest!" she exclaimed. "But how simply marvelous! I've been dying for years to meet a Catholic priest, but somehow there never seem to be any at any of the parties I go to. I've got such oodles and oodles to ask you that I don't know how I'll ever have time."

"Perhaps if you were to accompany me part of my way," Father Smith suggested. "I've got to return to my presbytery, I'm afraid."

"That'll be just too devastating," Miss Agdala said. "I like 'devastating,' don't you? Such a *crimson* word. Well, the first question I want to ask you is: Do you really believe it all, and if so, how?"

"I beg your pardon," Father Smith said as he walked heavily beside her fluttering frock. "Believe all what?"

"All that poppycock about Baptism and purity and the Virgin Birth, of course. My dear man, it's against all modern science and obstetrics."

"My dear young woman," Father Smith said, trying hard to keep his voice from trembling, "my dear young woman, I believe the poppycock about Baptism and purity and the Virgin Birth for the same reason as every other Catholic in the world believes them: because God has revealed them as facts, and not to believe them would be tantamount to telling God that He was a liar. And I do it by the simplest of all methods: firstly, by obedience, because God tells us to believe these doctrines; and, secondly, by logic, because it is only reasonable to suppose that He Who stuck in the stars and twirled the planets and tugged the tides can override the limitations that He Himself has imposed upon their movements. It is surely for Him Who hewed out Heaven to impose His own conditions of admittance, just as it is for Him Who worked out the mathematic of procreation and reproduction to omit the first step if He wants to. And a God Who has done such high things with flowers and trees and kittens' tails can surely give us His own Flesh to eat and His own Blood to drink in the Eucharist. For the miracle of rule and regulation is every bit as much a miracle as the miracle of the suspension of rule and regulation. It is just as much a miracle that your coat should hang where you put it last night as that it should fly to Siberia: for both, an act of God is necessary, an act of conservation or of transference. And as for purity, my dear young lady, that is God's business too, since He made children come that way and not daisies or buttercups."

"My dear Father, you really are a perfect case of sublimation," Miss Agdala said. "Shades of Freud and ghosts of Jung! But what do you do about sex yourself? How do you manage to live without *us*?"

"That is perhaps the easiest part of the religious life," Father Smith answered. "To begin with, touching daily the hem of His garment, priests do not see these things as other men do; and, to end with, women's bodies are rarely perfect; they soon grow old and sag, and always the contemplation of them even at their best is a poor and boring substitute for walking with God in His House as a friend; and they make themselves even more unattractive than they are by smearing and plastering and painting themselves until they cannot eat or drink without leaving the rust of their beauty on cups and napkins. I sometimes wonder, Miss Agdala, what a fashionable young woman would do if she awoke to find that her lips had turned permanently, overnight, the color she painted them. In any case, if I were pope, I think that I should commend the practice in an encyclical, because it makes women as unattractive as wet railings. But perhaps their conversation is the best antidote to priests seeking their society, because it is so inevitably frivolous, foolish, and boring." He spoke with such anger that he felt he really meant what he said.

"What you have just said proves what I have always maintained: that religion is only a substitute for sex," Miss Agdala said.

"I still prefer to believe that sex is a substitute for religion and that the young man who rings the bell at the brothel is unconsciously looking for God," Father Smith said.

"Read D. H. Lawrence if you don't believe me," Miss Agdala said. "Read any of the moderns. It's no use struggling against nature. People must be true to their chemistry. I'm a varietist myself." She rolled her eyes and swung her haunches as she spoke. "I may as well tell you once and for all that I don't believe in inhibitions," she said.

"Only in exhibitions, is that it?" Father Smith said, still finding it difficult to keep the rage and hurt in his soul from rocking his voice. "Well, let me tell you that Christ came into this world precisely in order to teach men how to struggle against the chemistries, if so you must call them, of desire and self-love. All through the ages, the Church of God has worked and prayed for this one end: to persuade men to obey Christ; its mission is and has always been and will always be an immense effort for a small effort: to storm, to threaten, to controvert, and to plead people into trying to correspond with sanctifying grace. Call the practice of this discipline an inhibition if you will. In that case, there is not only one inhibition but many, for Christ called men to refrain from murder and theft as well as from impurity. The Catholic Church, however, has another name for this obedience, because it is a rigor that makes saints."

"But who on earth wants to be a saint these days?" Miss Agdala asked.

"It is not what we want but what God wants," Father Smith said. He knew that there was a cleverer answer lying about his mind somewhere, but his anger was such that he could not lay his tongue to it. "God wants us to want to be saints," he said.

"My dear sir, you're a masochist, that's what you are," Miss Agdala said. "Like three-quarters of the rest of humanity, you are convinced that an action must be wrong if it's pleasant and that virtue consists in self-torture. Paganism is the only true philosophy, running carefree with bare loins across the golden sands of time, lusting with fair nymphs in the forest glades, for it is only when one has been impure that one is pure, because then and only then is one absolved from one's hormones."

"You do talk a lot of balderdash, don't you?" Father Smith said.

"I am happy if men account me a fool for Pan's sake," Miss Agdala said. "And yet it is not I who am the fool but you, because you still believe in the exploded fable of Christianity. Read Bertrand Russell, if you don't believe me; read Lytton Strachey; read Sinclair Lewis; we modern writers have debunked the old myths."

"Perhaps you have not read your contemporaries quite as intelligently as you imagine," Father Smith said, wishing that his holy religion did not forbid him to slap the young woman's face. "I shall tell you why. There are two kinds of agnostics: those who are sorry that they cannot believe the Christian revelation, because they realize both its beauty and its justice; and those who are glad that they need not believe it, because they can murder, steal, oppress, and lust without fear of punishment after death. It is to the former class that the majority of worthwhile modern writers appear to me to belong. When Lytton Strachey wrote of the flaws he found in Cardinal Manning's, Florence Nightingale's, General Gordon's, and Queen Victoria's characters, I am prepared to believe that he was actuated by no motive less worthy than a desire impartially to make known the truth. He erred, however, in two respects. As a clever man, he ought to have known that the surprising thing is not that a Cardinal Manning should be on occasion an ambitious and an unscrupulous man, but that an ambitious and an unscrupulous man should ever have been a Cardinal Manning. For it is a more astounding proof of God's grace that a sinner should raise himself to practice virtue than it is a proof of the inevitability of the devil's victory that a virtuous man should in an instance or two sink to sin. The second thing that he should have known was that the process of debunking, pursued from however lofty a motive, is in the end a danger to society. It is so because the majority of readers are so stupid that they do not see the moral end viewed by the author, that of knowing and making known the truth, but come instead to be persuaded that nobody in the whole world is inspired by a disinterested love of God or humanity, but that even the best men are consciously or unconsciously grafters and self-seekers, and that they themselves will be worse than fools if they do not become grafters and self-seekers too. Take Mr. Noel Coward, for instance, whose plays seem to be shocking people into paying him a fortune. I am quite persuaded that the young man is himself on the side of the angels and that his plays are written as sermons, but I am not at all convinced that that is the spirit in which the public goes to applaud them."

"You can say what you like, but Christianity has outlived its usefulness," Miss Agdala said as she stopped outside the Hotel Carlton-Elite and stood with her silk legs wide against the marble steps. With its windows like rows of snapshots in a photograph album, the hotel stretched and stretched and stretched.

"On the contrary, Christianity has not even begun to live its usefulness, and I doubt if it ever will, because God never promised that it would," Father Smith said.

"Communism is the only philosophy that will save the world," Miss Agdala said. "Did I tell you that I was a communist?"

Father Smith wanted to ask her if she gave all her royalties to the poor, but he didn't because he felt that it would have been too unkind, since a practicing communist could never have afforded to stay at the Carlton-Elite, where Oliver Ogilvie's Ohio Octette played "Yes, We Have No Bananas" to the nobs. Instead, he took off his hat and left her with the wind blowing her dress about her knees.

On the fringe of the damp slum of the pro-cathedral parish, he came upon Monsignor O'Duffy, who was standing outside a chemist's shop and blowing up balloons for a cluster of noisy urchins. The monsignor seemed to be enjoying himself enormously, for when he had blown up the balloons, he taught the children a song that he sang himself at them, beating time with his hands and bawling with gusto:

"I wish I was a bobby,
A big, fat bobby.
I'd wash my mither's lobby
Wi' washing sody."

"I've just been talking to the most objectionable young woman," Father Smith said as the monsignor and he waved their hands to the children and left them. "She's a novelist and imagines that she's discovered the secret of the universe, which is that there is no secret at all. That's the worst of all these moderns; they've no sense of the mystery. Now, Donne and Blake ..."

"Aye," said the monsignor, "give me good old Sexton any day of the week."

XVII

ALREADY IN MAY, 1926, when Father Smith went to admire Mother de la Tour's daffodils, there were lots of people walking, grown-up, about the town whom the priest did not remember ever having seen before. He supposed that it must be that the children were men and women now, only he thought it strange that he could no longer see the reflection of their infant chubbiness through the aggressive set of their eyes and chins. He himself was growing old, but he still seemed to see out of his face at the trams and the cobbles and the *People's Friend* posters in the same old way. On the bills outside his cinema, Signor Sarno was advertising Rudolph Valentino and Harold Lloyd, and the balcony seats had gone up to one-and-nine, but the priest did not pay much attention because the general strike was on, and policemen were walking about in groups, and sleek, young men of the upper classes were driving the trams.

Father Smith did not know quite what to make of the strike, because it seemed to him that the working people had a genuine grievance, only he didn't like the way they lounged about the town with their hands in their pockets. He didn't like the way the rich went about being loyal either, because he thought that it was easy for them to do poor men's work free for fun, and so he didn't know how to greet Lady Ippecacuanha when he came upon her, big, brassy, red-haired, and monocled, punching tickets and ringing the bell on the tram that was to take him from the presbytery to the convent.

"Dear Father Smith, I think it's simply marvelous the way everybody has been so loyal, don't you?" she boomed through her tusky teeth as she thrust a ticket upon him.

Loyal to what or to whom, Father Smith wondered, as he smiled foolishly back at her slice of face. Loyal to their bank balances, their dividends, and their dinner jackets or to their sense of Emmanuel, God-with-us? After all, it was as easy for Lady Ippecacuanha to be loyal as it was for Angus McNab to be disloyal. She had never sweated with fear in a trench, slept in mud, dared a sore, torn-apart death and been rewarded by having to hawk bootlaces on the street to the civilization she had helped to save. The immortal deeds of fame soon faded in men's memories, and the more immediate selfishness took their place. And was it right that the same people should go on being comfortable all the time? He was glad when the tram reached the convent and he was able to get off and walk away from Lady Ippecacuanha's make-thee-mightier-yet smile.

In the school, the children were practicing the sequence for Corpus Christi. Their young voices came out of the open windows to Father Smith as he walked on the lawn with Mother de la Tour:

> "Sit laus plena, sit sonora,
> Sit jucunda, sit decora
> Mentis jubilatio."

If only the whole world could sing such songs and mean them, there would be no more wars or unemployment or strikes or misery, Father Smith thought.

"Jamais la Révérende Mère ne vous pardonnera si vous n'allez pas leur dire un petit bon jour," Mother de la Tour said as she took up her watering can.

They were still singing when the priest entered the classroom. The big girls and the small girls were all there, wearing their white veils too, for they had been rehearsing the procession as well, when the bishop would carry the Blessed Sacrament along the path under the trees and they would walk with lighted candles in front of him. Mother Leclerc, who was choir-mistress, was conducting the singing while Reverend Mother sat on the dais beaming at them all through her spectacles.

> "Caro cibus, sanguis potus:
> Manet tamen Christus totus
> Sub utraque specie."

Reverend Mother waited until they had finished the whole sequence before she let Father Smith see that she was aware of his presence, and then she made him mount up onto the dais and said:

"Et maintenant, mes enfants, le Révérend Père Smith va bien vouloir nous dire quelque mots."

Feeling very foolish, as he always did when he had to speak in public in Reverend Mother's presence, Father Smith spoke briefly of the beauty of the great feast that they were about to celebrate. He told them that when they grew up and went out into the world, wicked men and women might try to make them forget the sweet doctrines that they had learned in the convent, but that they must not do so, because these doctrines were not only beautiful but true as well. One had only to hear the lovely hymn in honor of the Blessed Sacrament that they had just sung to realize that God had intended the world to be a great, golden place, and indeed He had made it such, because it was God Who had sculptured the mountains and hollowed the valleys and poured out the seas, while it was men who had bricked the cities, and that was why they were sometimes so ugly. The only time men had seemed able to create something really beautiful was when they had built the churches and cathedrals in the Middle Ages, and that was because they were thinking about God all the time they worked, and so lovely spires and stately steeples had come tapering out through their fingers. But they must always remember that no cathedral, no loch, and no mountain could ever be nearly as beautiful as our Lord in the Most Holy Sacrament of the Altar, as they would realize for themselves one day when they saw Him face to face in Heaven.

The children clapped a little when Father Smith had said this, but the priest was sure that they did so only out of politeness. It was impossible to tell from Reverend Mother's expression what she thought of his address. She did not tell him when they were alone together, either, but merely thanked him for his kindness in coming to see them and said Elvira had asked to be allowed to speak to him in the parlor.

Elvira was eighteen now. Standing, looking at the photograph of Cardinal Amette, late archbishop of Paris, she seemed older, but when she turned to greet him, the innocence of her face made her look younger.

"Buon giorno, carissimo padre mio," she greeted, and then her brave smile went and she flung herself upon the priest's shoulder, sobbing. "Per Bacco, but I am so miserable, Father, and nobody but you will understand. You see, I love him such a lot. Tell me, Father, is it wrong of me to love him when he is going away to learn to become a priest?"

Drawing her to a chair, Father Smith sat down beside her.

"Dear child," he said, "dear child, of course it is not wrong of you to love Joseph because he is going to become a priest. On the contrary, you should love him all the more because he is giving up everything for our Lord. But there are two kinds of love, Elvira: the earthly and the supernatural; and it is with the supernatural love that you must love Joseph."

"But if I never let him see that I love him with an earthly love?" she asked. "If I never hold his hand again or smile too much when I see him coming up the garden path?"

"Sweet child, you must learn to love him only in Christ," Father Smith said.

"But I love my *enemies* in Christ," Elvira protested. "I love them because our Lord died for them as He died for me; I love them because their bodies are temples of the Holy Ghost, just as my body is; I love them because God commands me to love them. But that is not the way I love Joseph. I love him that way too, of course, but I love him other ways as well. I love his eyes and I love his nose and I love his mouth and I love the way his hair grows. Tell me, Father: is it wrong for a girl to love the way a priest's hair grows?"

"If it is not wrong, at least it is dangerous," Father Smith said.

"Our Lord asks an awful lot of us at times, doesn't He?" Elvira said.

"We must remember that we shan't wake up in Heaven wondering how on earth we got there," Father Smith said, smiling inwardly to himself as he quoted Canon Bonnyboat's favorite thunder.

"I'm still going to be an actress, but when men turn to stare at me in the lounge of the Carlton-Elite, I'll still wish it was Joseph who was staring," Elvira said. "And I'll never, never marry anybody else, and I'll wear all my pretty clothes to the greater glory of God because Joseph will be too busy being a priest to be interested.

And every night I'll pray that God will grant him the grace of a happy death. Tell me, Father: if a girl can't love the way a priest's hair grows, surely she can still pray that God will grant him the grace of a happy death?"

"You'll grow out of your unhappiness, child, and in the meantime, the only thing you can do is to offer it up to God," Father Smith said as he left her. He felt that he ought to have been able to say something more consoling, especially when Elvira thanked him at the gate for having helped her so much.

Standing at the new traffic lights, James Scott, who had recently been promoted to pointsman, was controlling the arrival and the departure of the trams. With his now gray head growing up into his peaked blue cap, he blew one blast on his whistle for the trams to move into town and two blasts for them to move out of town. Crossing to congratulate him on not having gone out on strike, Father Smith wondered if he could have served the Lord as bravely as James Scott had done for the last twenty years if he had had to do it by punching tickets and blowing whistles. James Scott, however, did not seem to think that there was anything particularly brave in his not having gone out on strike, although he was manifestly pleased when Father Smith started to talk about Joseph and about how good a priest he thought the boy would make.

Thinking of one parishioner made Father Smith think of another, and so he decided that he would go and call on Angus McNab and see how the young man was getting on. He set out, therefore, along the mean streets that led to the slum where Angus and his wife lived. As he moved among the dirty children, he tried to smile at them as he thought Monsignor O'Duffy would have smiled at them, because he knew that it wasn't only clean children that God wanted priests to love but dirty ones especially, because they had so much to be compensated for; but he hadn't the monsignor's manner, because the children didn't smile back, and some of their parents even scowled, as though they were bracketing the priests with the employers. Father Smith began to wish that he had come another day, when there hadn't been a general strike, but he knew that was weak and cowardly of him.

He arrived at the tenement just in time to give Annie conditional absolution after Agnus had flung her out of the window. Kneeling on the pavement beside her broken body, he muttered the holy words while around him the stupid, hostile faces mooned. "Make an act of contrition," he exhorted the pulp and the blood and the matted hair. "Say: 'O my God, Who are infinitely good in Thyself …'"; but no words came back from the pulp and the blood and the matted hair, and the policemen were already upstairs to take Angus away.

XVIII

THEY HANGED ANGUS on the Feast of Saint Cyril of Jerusalem, 1927, so Father Smith had to wear white vestments where he went to say Mass and give him Holy Communion in his cell.

Angus's confession was like most other confessions Father Smith had heard, a long thread of repeated rebellions against God, the suck and swish and swirl of silly sins. At first, as he listened, the priest was too moved to pay much attention, because he was thinking of the dreadful thing that was going to happen to the young man and of how he himself was perhaps partly responsible, because he had told Angus in the trenches that the world was going to be a kind and just and holy place after the war; then he remembered that, as Cardinal Newman had pointed out, even the smallest of venial sins was, in the eyes of God, a greater evil than the destruction of the whole earth and the perishing of its inhabitants in agonies of torture, and he forced himself to listen carefully, so that when all had been said he might the more surely soothe with sacramental balm. For the world was "about" being good and being bad and not "about" trade winds and centers of depression and chemists' shops and the price of war loan, as deep down in their hearts most people knew, only they were afraid to say so out loud in case other people would laugh at them. Outside, as he thought this, the early morning trams clanged in the meaninglessness of another material day, and an early milk boy sang, "Charleston, Charleston, she told me that I couldn't dance the Charleston."

When he had given Angus absolution, Father Smith vested and began the Mass in front of the same little portable altar that he had used in France. Angus, who had insisted on serving, answered back with a great common Scots accent that lent pathos to his Latin: "Ad Deum, qui laetificat juventutem meam." And what joy had God given to Angus's youth? Father Smith wondered. Angus hadn't been happy at the war, and he hadn't been happy after the war, with no job and his trollop of a wife carrying on with other men as soon as his back was turned. But perhaps Angus had been happy as a boy, running with bare feet about the streets of the town. Perhaps he had been happy selling chocolates and cigarettes in Signor Sarno's cinema house. Or perhaps a glimpse of beauty had soaked color into his soul: the noise of the sea at night, the shine of the rain on a policeman's cape, the wreaths of incense still smudged about the altar when High Mass was over. A rage against the rich rose in the priest as he thought of how easy things had been for them and how difficult for Angus. It was so simple for them, with their green lawns and their limousines and their conservatories and their holidays at Dinard, to talk about what *they* would do if they were workingmen, but it wasn't so easy for the workingman, especially when he hadn't any work to do.

"Father, I'm that feared," Angus said when the Mass was over.

"Angus, when they come for you, you will say: 'Into Thy hands I commend my spirit; Lord Jesus, receive my soul,'" the priest said.

"Father, it's no right," Angus said. "She was a dirty, stravaiging whore and she deserved all she got and I'm no going to take it lying down."

"Angus, there'll be no peace in God's good world until taking things lying down becomes a contagion," the priest said.

"I'm no going to take things lying down, I tell you," Angus began to shout. "It's no right; it's no fair. I fought in the war, in the muck and the blood, aye for four lang years, with the wind cauld aboot ma belly, and my boots tramping on deid men's tripes and they stinking like sewer pipes. They'd won an immortal fame, their names'd be written on golden scrolls in great, big, red and purple letters, so the fellies that slept at hame in their beds said. And I'd won immortal fame too; my name ought to have been written on golden scrolls for folks to have a read at, because my guts might have been lying at the bottom of a trench too, all stretched oot and cauld and trampit doon. But folk had forgotten the war by the time I got hame, they'd forgotten the laddies that fought and died and bled oot their sair red blood for them, and the fellies that had stayed at hame were oot o' their beds now, rubbing their great randy bellies against the lassies in the paly de donces. And what did I get for risking my ain one life for them and what did I get for my poor sair arm? I didna get whooring aroond with the lassies, at least not with the stuck-up yins with their heids in the air and their silken doups that only farted lavender and eau-de-cologne, I didna; I got a job at thirty bob a week and Annie Rooney wi' a great muckle airse on her like Ben Nevis and a great cauld mooth, at least when I got pitten oot by yon Sarno for asking for forty bob instead of thirty it was. And yet I loved her, Faither, I loved her because I thought she was all my ain. That's why I went oot along the dreich clarty streets selling matches and bootlaces in the wind and the rain and the snaw. That's why I climbed all yon steep stane steps to try to sell pencils to scribbling writing men with wee peery eyes and great big nebs in their offices that didna care how many laddies' banes lay rotting in Flanders' fields so long as they were safe and alive and screwing oot their sneaky wee figures. And all the time, the dirty bitch was lying with her stinking meat in other men's airms with her yelly, yelly hair all streakit oot across the pillow and saying the same hot loving words in their lugs she used to say in mine. It's no fair, I tell you." Suddenly the venom was out of him, and he was sobbing in the priest's arms. "Faither, Faither, I'm that feared," he said.

"Angus, you mustn't talk like that," the priest said. "You're in a state of grace, remember, but you'll be out of it again before you know where you are if you go on like that. Don't forget the implications of Christianity, Angus. It was never intended to be an easy religion but a difficult one. That's just what the world doesn't understand, and yet it's precisely what our Blessed Lord came down from Heaven to teach. And He didn't find it easy to die either. Try to model yourself on Him, Angus. Try to understand something of the law of mystical substitution." He spoke quickly because he knew that time was short. "Make an act of contrition for the sins of your whole life, Angus. Tell God that you are sorry for not having understood His purpose better. Say: 'Into Thy Hands …'"; but already the warder was turning the key in the lock.

There were quite a few there to see Angus die: the governor, the magistrates, the doctor, the warders, the hangman, all neat and respectable in their boots, but the priest didn't look at them much because he was too busy holding up the crucifix to Angus and telling him to commend his soul to Jesus. When it was all over, he anointed the corpse, because he had not been able to do so previously as Angus had been in no technical danger of death. Then he went out into sad sunshine where a policeman was already pinning on the prison door the notice of Angus's death. The crowd of ghouls who had gathered on the pavement made way for him as they crammed forward to read the notice. Among them the priest

noticed Councilor Thompson, who surprisingly raised his hat.
Father Smith raised his hat back and then hurried home to the
church, where Canon Bonnyboat had promised to say the nine-
o'clock Mass for the repose of Angus's soul.

XIX

IN MAY, 1928, Mother de la Tour's wireless set was able to make such a noise that she didn't need any earphones to hear what the pretty girls were singing in London. But not all the noises it made were holy, so Reverend Mother suggested that it should be turned on as seldom as possible, although she admitted that she had no serious objection to "Tea for Two and Two for Tea," and "Rose Marie, I Love You," even if neither song contributed positively to the sanctification of souls. The films, too, were talking now, and Monsignor O'Duffy went so far as to predict that in another few years they would be stinking as well, but that didn't worry Signor Sarno, who had a nice lot of new names on the advertisements outside his cinema: gentlemen called R. Novarro and J. Gilbert, and ladies called C. Bennett and G. Garbo, all of whom were wows, but Miss G. Garbo especially, because of the superb way she could wear a mackintosh. The novelists, too, were in full song: John Galsworthy, Arnold Bennett, H. G. Wells, D. H. Lawrence, Aldous Huxley, Uncle Hugh Walpole, and all. In 1927, Gentlemen had Preferred Blondes, but now there was *The Bridge of San Luis Rey* and *All Quiet on the Western Front*, and everybody agreed that war was a very terrible scourge indeed, and the *Highland Herald* went even so far as to state that if bagpipes helped to arouse the martial spirit, then bagpipes ought to be shunned, sequestered, suppressed, and shattered in order that war might never, ever come again. Everywhere progress was on the upgrade and culture was having a boom: transatlantic flights, Al Capone, crossword puzzles, zip fasteners, contraceptives in slot machines, and contract bridge, and people began to feel a little sorry for the Greeks, who had only had Aristotle and Socrates and Plato, even though they had had a word for it.

The Church, however, still had her confessors, doctors, virgins, and martyrs, and although Saints Marius, Martha, Audifax, and Abachum were, for the moment, less well known than Harold Lloyd and Gloria Swanson, they looked as though they might last longer. So indeed thought Father Smith as he made his way one Friday afternoon to the convent to hear the nuns' confessions. Only that morning he had read in the *Daily Bugle* of a young American millionaire who employed to answer his social correspondence fifty typists, all of whom had to have red hair and pale green eyes. Interviewed in his favorite bathroom by a press representative, the millionaire had said: "I am a progressive. Freed from the shackles of superstition and dogma, I believe in the pulsation of life and in the elemental biologic principle. I want a good time, and as I've got the mazuma, why the heck shouldn't I have it?"

It didn't make sense to Father Smith, who had never been able to understand how people who split their infinitives, read Edgar Wallace for pleasure, and believed that black cats were unlucky should be intellectually insulted by the doctrine of transubstantiation; but then nothing ever did make sense in the *Daily Bugle*, which simultaneously held up for the admiration of its readers Steve Donoghue, Dean Inge, the Dolly Sisters, the Aga Khan, and Mrs. Aimée Macpherson.

The nuns' confessions always cheered Father Smith, because they made him realize that other people in the world were fighting the same lonely battle for grace. They also made him feel humble, because it was evident that the nuns were so much better at being holy than he was: they never lost their tempers, they never criticized their fellows, they never tried to jog God's elbow; they accepted their own tribulations and other people's imperfections as natural in this vale of tears. Listening to their swift French amid the smell of incense and old wood and clean linen, Father Smith often felt that it ought to have been he who should confess to them and not they to him.

He was always a little nervous when Reverend Mother came into the box, because he knew that spiritually she was ever so much better informed than he was and that he would need no end of help from the Holy Ghost if he were not to appear a fool when he gave her counsel. Today, however, she made him smile for the first time. Last Saturday, she had had occasion to address the girls of the junior school, who were aged from five to ten, and she had told them how very wrong it was for girls to put cosmetics on their faces because it was an insult to our Blessed Lord's handiwork, since if He had intended women's lips to be vermillion, He would have created them that color Himself. At the time, she had forgotten that she had been speaking to such very young girls, and now she wondered whether she had acted wisely or foolishly. Might she not have done more harm than good? Might she not inadvertently have encouraged some girls to contemplate a practice of which they had not heard until she had spoken of it to them? Bless her, Father, for she had sinned, but she would very much like Father Smith's advice on the subject.

Afterward, as they walked together in the garden, the priest was still smiling. He had given Reverend Mother an extra Hail

Mary to say "for spiritual indiscretion," and he was amused by the recollection. They paced up and down the flower beds in the smell of newly mown grass, and the rosary hanging from the Reverend Mother's girdle made a clicking wooden noise as she walked.

"Alors, mon père?" she asked, because she knew that the priest always liked to discuss with her the signs that he imagined he discerned in the outer world.

"God's Kingdom is not yet, ma révérende mère, but there are stirrings that are indicative of a change of spirit," he said.

Reverend Mother did not say anything but walked on with her hands folded beneath her scapular, waiting for the priest to continue.

"The people are foolish," Father Smith said. "They clamor for a new thing, but then they have always clamored for new things. Just now the new things are flying across the Atlantic, getting married by Protestant clergymen in diving suits at the bottom of swimming pools, or dancing for twenty-four hours on end without stopping, but one day, when the leaders of the world have learned wisdom and passed it on, the people will realize that there's much more fun to be had out of obeying God. And there are signs that the leaders of the world are waking up, or at least that the thinkers of the world are going to make them wake up. Two good books have been published: one is called *The Bridge of San Luis Rey* and the other is called *All Quiet on the Western Front*. The first is a beautiful book that sweetly shows forth the transcendent justice of Almighty God. It is, I think, encouraging that such a book should be a best-seller. The second is an ugly book, or perhaps it would be true to say that its subject matter is ugly, since it treats of war, its waste, and its futility. It was written by a German and is enjoying huge sales in all countries. Now, if only statesmen could be brought to understand that war is an evil but that it is not a necessarily recurrent evil. Tribal warfare has vanished. Why should not international warfare also vanish? Why should statesmen not be brought to realize that murder is no more justifiable when committed by a collectivity than when committed by an individual? Why should they not be brought to understand that a man who is wounded in the stomach suffers no less because another three hundred thousand men are simultaneously wounded in the stomach? And if wars can be banished from the earth, the opportunity for men to serve God will increase. I have always held that one of the reasons men fail so badly is that they do not live long enough to learn from their mistakes. Well, having no wars will be one way for humanity as a whole to live longer." He had uttered most of his speech down to the moving carpet of the grass, but now that he had finished, he looked up into Reverend Mother's wise, smooth face to see how she had taken it all.

"Mon père, I hope that you are right, but I am afraid that you are wrong," Reverend Mother said. "In all ages, there have been men who have dreamed of banishing wars, and they have always failed. They have failed because men will not obey God and love Him and their neighbors as themselves. War comes because of the absence of love, but that does not mean that love will come because of the absence of war. The Church has always been buffeted by many winds, mon père: by the hatred of her enemies, by the disobedience of her children, by the ambition of her less worthy prelates. And I think that she will always be so buffeted because it is only in Heaven that our Lord has promised that the Church will be triumphant. In the meantime, we can only pray and thank Almighty God that green grass smells so sweet and hope that it will smell as sweet in Heaven."

"But we must act as well, ma révérende mère, we must cooperate with sanctifying grace," Father Smith said.

He felt that he could have gone on talking to Reverend Mother for hours yet, but Mother Leclerc came out across the lawn in her flopping black habit and said that they must both come into the parlor at once and see Elvira Sarno's new photograph that had just arrived from America, from a place called Hollywood.

Elvira had been in America for more than a year now, and Father Smith wanted very much to see her photograph, but he wanted even more to tell Reverend Mother that in his opinion the leaders of the Church had grown so used to the spectacle of the world neglecting the wisdom of Christ that they had ceased to be shocked by it and that what was wanted was a renewal of the apostolic spirit among cardinals and archbishops and papal nuncios. It was no use preaching the gospel only to those who came to church to hear it. The gospel ought to be preached to those who didn't want to hear it as well: to industrialists in their offices, to clubmen in their windows, to workers in their yards and factories, to bibbers in their taverns, to harlots in their doorways, to all those should the sweet tidings of Christ be taught. It was a sorry matter for reflection that it was only heretics who dared to brave the sneers of the mob by crying aloud the Name of Jesus at street corners and in the marketplace. All this he wanted to say to Reverend Mother, but Mother Leclerc kept chattering away beside them about how beautiful Elvira was in her photograph and not nearly as worldly-looking as she had feared, and in any case, it was rather a complicated sequence of sentiments for him to put into immediate French.

Elvira did, indeed, look beautiful on her glossy photograph on which she had written in the corner: "To my dear, sweet nuns, in memory of many happy yesterdays. Elvira Sarno." Reverend Mother held the photograph up to the light and examined it attentively, and Father Smith knew that she was scrutinizing the eyes for the evidence of compromission with the world. He, too, examined the photograph closely: the shiny lips looked almost black, and the eyebrows seemed strangely thin, but the eyes were the same eyes that he had seen gazing starrily across the altar rail at her First Communion.

"We shall have the photograph framed and hung in the parlor," Reverend Mother decided.

"But will his lordship the bishop approve?" Mother Leclerc asked. "Je sais qu'elle est ravissante, mais elle est tout de même actrice, et ma mère m'a toujours dit que les actrices c'étaient tout de même des actrices, et puis il y a déjà la photographie de Sa Sainteté."

"His lordship will approve, because he knows just as well as I do that it is possible to act as well as to stoke furnaces or to pray to the greater glory of God," Reverend Mother said. "And I am sure that His Holiness wouldn't mind either. Elvira Sarno was our pupil, and she is now our friend. Even if she has chosen a dangerous profession, it is our duty to pray for her, that she may carry into strange places the lamp we lighted for her here. And even if she fails, it will still be our duty to pray for her, so that she may become again the child she was when she was at this school."

Father Smith felt that he could have kissed Reverend Mother for this speech. Instead, he said that he thought that he had at the presbytery the very frame to fit the photograph. At present it held the image of a friend of his who had recently become a Vicar Apostolic in Basutoland, but he didn't think the Vicar Apostolic would mind giving up the frame to Elvira, especially as the photograph was very faded now. In any case, he would bring the frame along tomorrow. Reverend Mother and Mother Leclerc said that that was very kind of Father Smith, and Mother Leclerc added that perhaps Elvira would one day bring great honor to them all by acting in a film the part of Bernadette Soubirous or Saint Teresa of the Child Jesus or Saint Margaret Mary Alocoque, or even our Blessed Lady herself.

When he was happy, Father Smith always sang snatches from the psalms as he walked along the street. Today as he returned to the presbytery he sang the "Magnificat." He was so pleased about what Reverend Mother had said about Elvira that he almost bawled the verses: "Magnificat anima mea Dominum. Et exsultavit spiritus meus in Deo salutari meo." People turned to stare at him as he passed, but the priest was too elated to notice and kept right on to the end, shouting his gratitude up to God, thundering Latin, false notes and all: "Sicut locutus est ad patres nostros: Abraham et semini eius in saecula." When he stopped, he found himself in front of Signor Sarno's cinema. The proprietor himself was standing on the steps, airing his three rings of chin.

"Buona sera, reverendo padre mio," Signor Sarno greeted. "You come see my little girl act. Very nice. Very moving. In the bathrooms scene she is especially magnificent. Very passionate, very pure. 'Bill,' she says, 'you get to Hell out of it or I'll throw you out on your ear,' and then she has her bath and sings 'Ave Maria' just to show she ain't no floosie. You pop in for a look-see, reverendo Father. I stand you exquisitely upholstered seat."

Father Smith wondered why it was that he hadn't noticed the name, Elvira Sarno, on the bills, but he supposed that it must be because down the years he had seen so many names from Hoot Gibson to Tom Mix larded up there that he had ceased to pay any real attention to them. All the films seemed to have similar titles and to deal with similarly trivial problems, such as whether a wife could run an advertising agency and yet be at her brightest and best when she dined downtown with her stockbroker husband.

The title of Elvira's film did not sound very profound either: *Love for an Hour*. Because he wished at all costs to be able to go on believing in Elvira, the priest decided that he would not accept her father's invitation. He knew that it was cowardly of him, but he consoled himself by remembering that Monsignor Robert Hugh Benson had always refrained from reading the New Testament in Greek in case the exercise would destroy his faith.

Signor Sarno seemed disappointed when Father Smith declined his offer, but he brightened when, out of politeness, the priest asked him if he thought that conditions were better in Italy after six years of fascist rule.

"Questo Mussolini è il piu gran uomo di stato del mondo," he said. "He has made of my country an ordered house. No more bits of dirty paper lying about the streets, no more late trains, only in-time trains. And soon he will make of it a powerful country as well. In ten years' time we shall have a population of sixty million people, sesanta milioni d'abitanti, reverendo Father, and then these dirty Frenchmen can look out for their skins. And in the meantime, we prepare. In my country the sale of *All Quiet on the Western Front* has been prohibited, because in fascist Italy we know that no country can be great without war. 'The nineteenth century has been the century of our freedom, but the twentieth century will be the century of our power,' so Mussolini says. Evviva il Duce!"

Father Smith told Signor Sarno then and there, and as blisteringly as was consistent with his priestly calling, just how great a book he thought *All Quiet on the Western Front* and how ignoble the ambitions of Mussolini, who ought to understand that the true grandeur of nations, as of individuals, came from their souls and not from their possessions; but Signor Sarno merely smiled and shook his head as he had smiled and shaken his head when the priest had asked him to take Angus McNab back unto employment.

Crossing the road to the presbytery, Father Smith sang no more psalms, because his heart was heavy within him that even great men could be so foolish. Outside the presbytery door itself, a beggar stopped him and asked for alms. He did not look sincere, but the priest gave him a shilling, which he couldn't afford, because Monsignor O'Duffy always maintained that it was a Christian's duty to risk giving wrongly rather than to risk sending one truly representing our Lord away empty.

XX

FATHER SMITH WAS sixty-one years of age when, in 1929, the bishop made him a canon of the pro-cathedral, reinstated him as rector of the Church of the Holy Name, and transferred Canon Bonnyboat to Saint Mungo's, Strathtochter. Monsignor O'Duffy was jubilant and said that it just showed ye that everything came to him who waited, and that the nuns at the convent would cheer like a crowd at a football match when they saw him daundering into the sanctuary in a purple cassock. And on the Feast of Saints Marcellinus, Peter, and Erasmus, Martyrs, Thomas Edmund Smith sang his first capitular High Mass in the pro-cathedral, with Canon Muldoon as deacon and Canon Bonnyboat as subdeacon, and Monsignor O'Duffy himself as master of ceremonies.

As it was a weekday, the congregation was small, with Lady Ippecacuanha very prominent in the front row. The canons, however, were all there, fitted into their stalls like pipes into racks, and Canon Smith felt very nervous because he knew that his voice, never good at any time, was now old and cracked. The collect bothered him quite a lot, and he decided to sing it on a low tone so that his faults might be the less noticed; but before he had got the first clause out, Monsignor O'Duffy, who was standing beside him, whispered: "Sing oot louder, Tam; the auld wives at the back'll no be able tae hear ye."

When the Mass was over, the chapter meeting took place in the presbytery because there was no proper chapter house. Shorn of their vestments and their robes, the successors of Saint Andrew and Saint Kentigern and Saint Blaan and Saint Drostan and Saint Columba sat round the somber dining room in their square black boots and alpaca jackets that came halfway down their thighs. Christopher Canon Bonnyboat of Saint Mungo's, Strathtochter; Aloysius Patrick Francis Canon Muldoon of the Sacred Heart, Drumfillans; Peter Canon Dobbie of Our Lady, Help of Christians, Abergirnie; James Canon Sellar of the Five Wounds, Kilngavie; Francis Xavier Canon Poustie of the Immaculate Conception, Lochmuchtyhead; Thomas Edmund Canon Smith of the Church of the Holy Name — they were all there, men with old faces and young eyes, butchers, bakers, and candlestick makers stilled into priests. Through the open windows came the caw of gulls and the happy cry of children as they played by the June sea.

When Monsignor O'Duffy had opened the meeting with prayer, Canon Poustie rose and asked the chapter what, in their opinion, was the best way of dealing with lovers when found canoodling in church doors. He said that it was his practice to go round the outside of his church with a flash lamp after Benediction each evening and chase the lovers out of the buttresses and off the porch, but that it didn't seem to do much good, because the shameless creatures just crossed to the Baptist church on the opposite side of the road and carried on their iniquitous practices there. Canon Dobbie said that he fully sympathized with Canon Poustie, because there were always lovers cramming onto the porch of the Church of Our Lady, Help of Christians, Abergirnie, too, but that he had come to the conclusion that it was best to leave them where they were, as it was just as possible that a grace from the Blessed Sacrament might touch their souls as that the tempo of their embraces might offend the Blessed Sacrament.

Monsignor O'Duffy then rose and said that he thought that Canon Dobbie's answer to Canon Poustie was a very beautiful and consoling one, and that none of them must ever forget that God moved in a mysterious way, and that the Blessed Sacrament was a very wonderful sacrament, indeed, and could shoot out all sorts of graces, even through stone and lime, at people who hadn't the slightest idea that Jesus Christ Himself was within a million miles of them. Perhaps, though, his old friend, Canon Smith, whom they were all delighted to welcome among them, would like to say a few words on the subject.

"Right Reverend and Very Reverend Fathers," Canon Smith began, "I thank Monsignor O'Duffy for his very kind reference to me. I think, though, that Canon Dobbie is right when he suggests that we should leave the lovers to our Lord, because the sacraments are powerful in these matters and because the Church's teaching thereon is well known. Indeed, so well known, even among heretics and schismatics, is the Church's teaching on sexual morality that it is popularly supposed that the word sin connotes almost exclusively the grosser carnal misdemeanors and that lack of charity is a peccadillo that our Lord will pardon easily. Please do not misunderstand me. I am not trying to minimize or to excuse in any way the conduct of which Monsignor O'Duffy and Canon Poustie complain. I am aware of the deep offense that such behavior gives to our Blessed Lord, and I fully understand that no adulterer or fornicator can readily apprehend the spiritual truths of our holy religion. But for Catholics, there are the sacraments to cool them; and even to non-Catholics, our teaching is, I repeat, well known, so that anything in the nature of a special campaign would, I think, be a work of supererogation.

"There are, however, other matters to which I think we priests might profitably give our attention. A French agnostic once asked, 'Si Dieu a parlé, pourquoi le monde n'est-il pas convaincu?' God, we know, has spoken, and, equally we know, the world is not convinced. It cannot, we also know, be the Church's fault that the world is not convinced, since the Church is guided by the Holy Ghost and is the infallible depository of those truths that Almighty God has chosen to reveal; but it may conceivably be the fault of churchmen who have stressed some of those truths at the expense of others that they have scarcely stressed at all.

"One of the reasons that the world is not convinced is, I think, that men believe that the Church, which they confuse with churchmen, teaches a short-range rather than a long-range morality. They hear the adulterer, the thief, and the murderer condemned from our pulpits, but not the employer of sweated labor, not the shareholder in armaments factories, not the men who make their money out of films about gangsters, not the politicians who compromise with the perpetrators of cruelty in faraway lands. They argue that, in the eyes of the Church, a man who owns shares in a company that makes its profits through underpaying Chinese workers is a good Christian so long as he doesn't murder the friend who beats him at golf or cohabit with his parlor maid. We, who are priests, know that this is not the teaching of the Church, but can we honestly say that we have taken the trouble to let men of good faith know that this is not the teaching of the Church? For, as is evident, many men of good faith remain outside the Church. Is it not for us to ask ourselves if we have not, by condemning only those sins that it takes little courage to chasten, prevented them from finding their way into the Fold that is Christ's?

"Right Reverend and Very Reverend Fathers, there are more than three hundred million Catholics in the world today belonging for the most part to the civilized nations of Europe. What an influence for good could we not exercise if each one of those three hundred million Catholics were an ardent follower of Christ, ready to put the teaching of his holy religion before interests of self or country. Instead of that, whom do we find? We find that heretics and schismatics, even atheists, are claiming to practice a charity more perfect than ours. For what else is the communist heresy but the boast to be able to love one's fellow man without first loving God? Right Reverend and Very Reverend Fathers, I speak in all seriousness. The Church of God cannot fail, but churchmen can and will delay her success unless they call the faithful back to the practice of rigorous and uncompromising religion. We must be pure, yes, because fornicators shall not clearly see God. We must be humble too, because our virtue is so frail. But above all, we must be brave and cry aloud to men to practice virtues that are more unpopular than purity and humility. We must tell them that a lot of things, which apparently have nothing to do with Christianity, have everything to do with Christianity. We must make them understand that modern advertising is a sin against God as well as against good taste, because it seduces the senses from an appreciation of Him and teaches men to love that which is shoddy and vulgar and temporal. We must teach men that ugly animals can suffer as sharply as beautiful animals, that an insect can feel agony as acutely as a hippopotamus, that a million men who die in battle are a million lonelinesses, each separate and alone with stars and trees and woods. We must teach men that wrong is not right because a community practices it. We must insist that the so-called useless subjects be taught in our schools, since it is not the poets who make wars. In short, Right Reverend and Very Reverend Fathers, we must try to save the world from another war while there is yet time, and there is only one way to do that: by preaching the full, fearless doctrine of Christ, by teaching the religion *of* Jesus as well as the religion *about* Jesus, by proclaiming that God wants men to be just and kind to one another as well as to believe that He is really and truly present in the Sacrament of the Altar. In that way will the raiment of the Bride of Christ shine white for all men to see, because our faith shall be justified by our works; for doctrine without charity is only less dangerous than charity without doctrine."

Sitting down, Father Smith saw at once that they had not understood. He saw it from the way they avoided his gaze and looked sideways at one another when they thought that he wasn't looking. Even Monsignor O'Duffy and Canon Bonnyboat seemed perturbed and unhappy. And yet all of them when they had been young had seen the vision and followed it and become priests. They had known then that security and prosperity were mean goals and that the achievement of sanctity was the only thing that mattered. Even although none of them were saints behind their tired faces, they must still know that it was the duty of all men to try to be saints, for they were priests, humble men highly set apart. Why, then, hadn't they understood when he had called upon them to see again the City of God they must all have glimpsed on the day of their ordination? Was it that their piety had become a habit, or was it that his own words had been badly chosen? He was still puzzling over this when Canon Sellar rose.

"When a bishop pontificates at the ceremonies on Holy Saturday, ought he to remove his miter when lying prostrate in front of the altar during the litany of the saints?" he asked.

XXI

THE BISHOP WAS sixty-eight years of age now and still very active, although he wasn't quite as good at getting out of the way of tramcars and buses as he used to be. Indeed, so wearying had walking and traveling become to him that he had bought an Austin seven in which he was able to visit not only the various churches in the town but a great number of those in the surrounding countryside as well. Although what he spent in petrol he economized in railway fares, the bishop sometimes felt guilty as he drove about his diocese and wondered if our Lord could really countenance such worldliness.

Two days after Canon Smith's speech at the chapter meeting, his lordship had a puncture driving along the High Street. Suppressing an exclamation of impatience, because he was on his way to administer the sacrament of Confirmation to three black medical students and a corporal of the Argyll and Sutherland Highlanders at Abergirnie, he got out and was preparing to unscrew the spare wheel when Canon Smith passed and, seeing the bishop's plight, offered to aid him.

"That is most kind of you, Canon," the bishop said. "I am afraid that I am one of those who drive a car implicitly rather than explicitly. Carburetors and sparking plugs and cylinders are mysteries that I accept on the authority of my garage proprietor; and even so comparatively simple a matter as changing a wheel tries my mental faculties almost as sorely as my physical."

"It's quite simple really," Canon Smith said. "First you raise the back wheel on the jack."

"I rather think I've got a tool like that somewhere, only I must confess that I always thought that it was called a william," the bishop said.

Meanwhile, a crowd had gathered on the pavement to watch the unusual spectacle of two elderly clergymen changing a wheel on a car. With open mouths and mooning eyes they stared, but none of them offered to help. The bishop wanted to unscrew some of the bolts that kept the spare wheel in position himself, but Canon Smith refused to relinquish the spanner.

"Talking about war, we mustn't forget that the Church has always taught that it is legitimate to fight in defense of one's country," the bishop said gently as he watched the canon's fingers nimbly untwisting the bolts.

The punctured rear wheel was well clear of the ground now. Canon Smith took the spanner again and began to loosen the next octagon of bolts. The crowd watched on with concentrated apathy.

"I don't deny that, my lord," Canon Smith said. "But there would be no need to defend one's country if the spirit of conquest and aggression were to be rooted out from the world. And then, with nation mistrusting nation, it is so difficult to say who is the aggressor and who is the defender. And, surely, my lord, it is the duty of priests to preach a wider charity. There is something revolting and hideous in millions of men learning to hate and to kill millions of other men they have never seen. For men are much of a mediocrity, my lord, be they British, German, Russian, French, or Spanish: vaunters about what they can't do, humble about what they can; liars in safety, truthful in danger; cowardly in smoke-rooms and brave in shell-holes; lewd with strange women and tender with their wives; hating the misery they can't see and succoring that which they can; stupid with books and clever with spanners; all with bellies and all alone with the stars and the sky not caring; all so very pitiful when you see them asleep; and all stamped in God's image, all fearfully and wonderfully made, all with eyelashes and fingernails and ears. Surely it is the Church's duty to make them love one another."

"The trouble with you, Canon, is that you are a poet," the bishop said, but he did not say it unkindly. "Perhaps that is why you are so impatient. Perhaps, too, you are unduly pessimistic. And remember that our Blessed Lord Himself said: 'Multi enim sunt vocati, pauci vero electi.' And the essential difference between Christianity and other religions is that Christianity is a difficult religion. It is not easy for men to abandon pleasure and prosperity and power and live each day as though it were their last. It never has been, and it never will be. Bearing this in mind, the Church is patient as God behind His screen is patient. She is patient because she knows that men are not converted by argument alone but by God's grace as well; she is patient because she knows that she carries a great responsibility: that of saving down the ages the greatest possible number of human souls; but above all, she is patient because she knows that she will ultimately triumph, because Christ has promised that she will.

"So with her pharmacy of sacraments she waits, healing as many souls as possible, preaching the startling truth that whosoever shall lose his life shall find it, controverting, carrying the cross into strange lands, pleading, condemning, threatening, but always aware that she must not unnecessarily give offense lest she lose souls for Almighty God. That is why she makes pacts and agreements with heathen and heretical governments, that she may distribute the Bread of Life as widely as possible and succor her many children in strange lands. And that is why in times of war she is impartial, because she knows that no nation perfectly practices righteousness and that the rulers of all nations are proud and blown out with vain ambitions. For the Church, Canon Smith, is very old and wise, and she has preached the gospel in ice and fire and heat and snow. It does not astonish her that there should be sin and disorder in the world; rather is she astonished that there should also be virtue and order. And she knows, because she reads reality in God's mirror, that there is one thing that is worse than a million young men dying on the field of battle, and that is one old man dying in his bed in a state of final impenitence. And now I am afraid that I must fly or I shall be very late indeed. That's right, Canon. Just put the william back in the toolbox."

Canon Smith knew that he had been rebuked for what the bishop no doubt considered an excess of zeal, and he felt very humble, because he knew that the bishop was a much holier man than he.

"I am sorry if any words of mine should have given offense, my lord, but I assure you that I was genuinely troubled by certain signs in the world and still am," he said.

"The answer to all our troubles is to carry out the old, old duties of our priesthood patiently," the bishop said. "And remember that we are always wise at the altar, because there God gives us the words and guides our hands. And talking about the priesthood, I am thinking of sending you young Joseph Scott as a curate when he's ordained."

Canon Smith knew that he was forgiven when the bishop said this, because the bishop was as fond of the young man as he was.

With his hat in his hand, he stood smiling as the bishop drove off in a snort and a puff of pale blue smoke. The crowd mooched away in sullen disinterest, but the canon still stood there smiling, thinking how wise the bishop was and how proud and ill-informed himself. It was not until later that evening that he remembered how wrong the bishop had been about the good that was going to come out of the last war, but he put the thought away from him, because he wanted very much to believe that the bishop was right now.

XXII

FATHER JOSEPH SCOTT was ordained priest by the bishop in the pro-cathedral on the Feast of Saint Peter and Saint Paul, 1932, and said his first Mass the next day in the chapel of the convent, because the nuns had asked for him to say it there, as he had learned his first lessons from them as a little boy. Lilies and roses from Mother de la Tour's garden had been banked on and about the altar, and the white flag of Henri IV, of François I, and of Joan of Arc had been hoisted at the gates, as the nuns didn't like the tricolor anymore, now that the religious orders had been driven out of France. The children of the junior school were to make their First Communion, the bishop himself was to preach a special sermon, and, unknown to Reverend Mother, Mother Leclerc had smuggled the parrot up with her into the organ loft, because she thought that even an animal ought not to be allowed to miss the edifying ceremony of a newly ordained priest saying Holy Mass for the first time.

The bishop and Monsignor O'Duffy and Canons Bonnyboat and Smith all met in the sacristy and helped Father Scott to put on the heavy, old, red chasuble that had once been worn by the Curé d'Ars, now called Saint Jean Vianney, and that had been laid out specially by the nuns. As soon as they entered the chapel,

Mother Leclerc began to play the "Ecce Sacerdos Magnus." It was a good thing she knew the score by heart, because she was crying so much that she couldn't read the music as she was playing it for Father Scott as well as for the bishop; but the children didn't know the words well, because they had learned them only the previous week, and they broke down when they came to "Non est inventus similis illi, qui conservaret legem excelsi," but Mother Leclerc knew it didn't really matter, because Almighty God heard all right. As they walked down the aisle, the bishop scattered little blessings to right and to left, because he was their Father-in-God, their good and wise pontiff.

After the Gospel, with its appropriate counsel, "Ecce ego mitto vos sicut oves in medio luporum. Estote ergo prudentes sicut serpentes et simplices sicut columbae," Father Scott left the altar, and the bishop spoke out over the nuns' coifs, which were riding the pews like gulls on waves.

The priest who was saying Mass for the first time today and the children who were going to receive their first Holy Communion at his hands must always remember, the bishop said, that far greater than the marvels of trains and airplanes and wireless telegraphy was the miracle of the Blessed Sacrament, in which Jesus came and came again in a clean, white wind. The continuance of this miracle down the ages had been secured by the Sacrament of Holy Orders, by which bishops and priests and deacons were consecrated and ordained for God's work. Before our Lord had ascended into Heaven, He had given power to His apostles not only to forgive sins and to turn bread and wine into His Body and Blood as He Himself had done at the Last Supper in the upper room, but also to transmit those holy powers to other men so that the sacraments might go on and on across continents and through jungles and down past kings and queens as they grew old and died, and past popes, too, sliding away down over the windows of empires and kingdoms and republics in a lovely rope of silver and gold. That rope was known to theologians as the apostolic succession; and each time that a bishop ordained a priest, there blew down from Heaven a great gust of Holy Ghost that inflated the ordinand's soul with the same powers as our Lord had breathed upon the apostles when He had commanded them to go and teach all nations whatsoever things He had commanded them. The nuns began to weep as the bishop said this, but they weren't weeping because they were sad but because they were happy, because a new priest had been given to God.

Father Scott's father and mother were the first to receive Holy Communion at the young priest's hands, as was only fitting, since they had given him to God. Mr. Scott wore his tramwayman's blue uniform for the occasion because he had to go out on points duty immediately afterward, but his wife had bought a new hat, all yellow and green and blue and red. Then came Father Scott's brothers and sisters, all the steps and stairs of them, and then the children in their lovely white dresses, and then the nuns with grave faces and folded hands. Last of all came a tall, dark, lovely young woman whom Canon Smith didn't recognize as Elvira Sarno until it was all over and Father Scott had prayed to Holy Michael, the Archangel, to deliver them on the day and to thrust down to Hell Satan and all wicked spirits who wandered through the world for the ruin of souls.

XXIII

ELVIRA HADN'T FORGOTTEN the Church of the Holy Name while she had been away in America, making a fortune, telling Clark Gable and Franchot Tone to step on it, Steve, and entertaining the Misses Dietrich, Harlow, West, Rogers, and Loy at her palatial residence in Beverly Hills. She gave the canon a check for five thousand pounds so that he could build a real stone church, as the old tin one was beginning to leak. The canon, when he had thanked her, said that he would build the new chancel first, as this was the most important. She also brought him for High Mass six sets of vestments in all the colors of the Roman sequence, including pink for *Laetare* and *Gaudete* Sundays. For this the canon was very grateful, because the green chasuble with the lamb on the back, which, from a distance, looked like a horse, was beginning to get rather faded. Elvira hadn't forgotten the nuns at the convent either, for she had brought them vestments as well, white, red, green, purple, and black, and a gold monstrance set with rubies and sapphires. She also invited the canon to lunch with her at the Carlton-Elite, because she said that she wanted to have a heart-to-heart talk with him.

Canon Smith hadn't been in the Carlton-Elite since five years previously, when he had taken the last sacraments to a dying

Portuguese admiral, and he found the vestibule very worldly, with painted young women standing about with their overcoats thrown loosely over their shoulders and smoking with aggressive venom as though they were doing something both wicked and complicated, like committing adultery in Russian. The men who were with them all seemed to have sallow faces and wide trousers and suede shoes and to be talking about a tip a broker johnny had given them that morning or what sort of time old Charlie had had at Monty. Used to contemplating sin and futility only from the pulpit and the confessional, the canon was appalled when he met them on the same carpet, and, in order not to be obliged to inspect them too closely, he crossed to the bookstall, which was piled with *Magnolia Street* and *The Fountain*.

"Buon giorno, carissimo padre mio; mi scusi di averla fatto aspettare." Elvira, the priest saw as he turned to greet her, was also wearing her overcoat thrown loosely over her shoulders, and so he concluded that the affectation couldn't be so wicked after all. "Per Bacco," she added, not because it was appropriate but just to make his old, tired face laugh.

"Per Bacco, ma sei veramente incantevole," Canon Smith said with a gallantry that was as sincere as it was unwonted.

"That's not at all the sort of thing that a holy man of God should say to a cinema star," Elvira said as she led him into the cocktail lounge.

For all his sixty-four years, the canon had never been in a cocktail lounge before, but Monsignor O'Duffy had told him that they were places where men and women who didn't believe in the Trinity forgathered to make lewd merriment over outlandish brews and potations. He looked about him with interest, therefore. All over the room the same patterns of pink-putty people as he had seen parading in the vestibule were sitting about at small tables drinking tight little lakes of colored drinks out of glasses with long stems. Certainly none of them seemed to be dressed in such a way as to suggest that they believed very ardently in the Trinity, and some of the brews and potations they were consuming looked as though they might, indeed, be outlandish, but the canon didn't see any signs of merriment, lewd or innocent. Instead, there were hopelessness, envy, and disappointment in their unlighted eyes, although they stretched their lips politely and showed great teeth like horses when their companions spoke to them. Alone against the wall on the other side of the room, a fat little bald man pulled out a thick gold watch, held it to his ear, and put it back into his pocket again.

When the waiter came and asked them what they wanted to drink, the canon was at a loss what to say, because there were so many names he didn't know to choose from: martinis, manhattans, bronxes, angel's kisses, and sidecars; but Elvira helped him out and said that she thought that they'd both better have a sidecar.

The strange drink when it came looked rather like soapy water, but Elvira said that it tasted much nicer than it looked, and indeed it did, and after a sip or two the canon began to be able to believe that the tweed suits and fur coats and high heels and silk stockings all around weren't perhaps as worldly as they looked and might even love our Blessed Lord a little, provided there was an organ playing.

"Are you happy, child?" he asked at length.

"When men stare at me, I still wish it was he that was staring," she said. "When we go into the dining room in a minute, men will turn and stare again, and I'll still wish that it was he who was staring. And all I can do is to pray that God will give him the grace of a happy death, which he is pretty certain to have in any case as he is a priest. But there's nothing to be afraid of, Father," she said, observing his worry. "In these matters, it takes two to make a danger. Why, Joseph scarcely knows that I exist now. Do you know what he said to me in the sacristy this morning when I went to give him my good wishes? 'Oh, hello, Elvira. Nice to see you again. You're on the stage or in opera or something, aren't you?' "

"You must remember that the study of the contemporary cinema is not encouraged in seminaries," Canon Smith said.

They finished their drinks in silence and then rose and went into the dining room. As Elvira had predicted, people turned to stare at her, but the canon could not make out whether it was because she was beautiful or because they knew that she was a famous cinema actress. The headwaiter showed them to a table at the window, with a view of the tramways passing, all plastered with advertisements and tiny people hurrying. At the next table, four red-faced businessmen were swilling down gin and Italians and talking with loud jocosity.

"We'd better order a dozen of these things each and have done with it," one of them said as he gulped with relish. "Waiter, another four same agains and look slippy about it."

"Now this johnny Hitler," another of them said.

"What johnny Hitler?" another of them asked.

"He means the chap who's trying to form a new party in Germany," another of them said.

"Just a flash in the pan, that's all," the first man said. "All these continental politicians are alike: they never last. And in any case, who wants to worry about Germany? We licked her, didn't we?"

"This chap Hitler says he's out to make Germany strong and powerful again," the second man said.

"Well, if there's another war, all I can say is I'm waiting till they come and fetch me," the third man said. "Look at what the last one did to us: messed up business and now there's no money left for anybody."

"He's a fine one to talk," the fourth man said. "Made a nice little packet the other day, he did."

"Now look here, Jimmy, just because I bought the missus a new Daimler. And what about Harry here with his Rolls?"

A gentleman with a nose like a purple pumice stone and mean little piggy eyes raised his glass benevolently in the air.

"I've always maintained that all this talk about a slump was demoralizing," he said. "Talk about a slump and chaps tread on your ear. Don't talk about a slump and keep your optics skinned, and before you know where you are, you're in the dough."

"All the same, you can't deny that there's serious unemployment in the country," Jimmy said.

"Sheer damned laziness if you ask me," Harry said. "Now if I were a shipwright and there was no work for me in the shipyards, I'd walk the country till I found work on a farm or down a mine or humphing luggage on barrows in a railway station. Wouldn't matter what it was so long as it was good, honest work. But no; the modern workingman isn't like that: he prefers to sit at home and draw the dole. And who's paying for it? The same old mutts, of course: you and me. It's just as well the company's had a good year."

"I say, Tom, what did you say that German chap's name was?" the third man asked.

"You mean Hitler," Tom answered. "Aitch-aye—damn it, Andrew, I can't remember whether there are two tees or only one. Waiter, another four same agains."

Elvira and the canon had just finished ordering their lunch when across the square came a procession of tattered men with banners. They were the unemployed shipyard workers marching out to call on the prime minister in London. Lean and haggard and with angry eyes they came, shuffling, out-of-step, dank, dreary, and dirty. Some of them wore their war medals on their breasts, and some of them had great cracked boots with socks and sometimes toes showing through, and some of them raised a clenched fist as they passed the hotel windows. Two tables away from the canon, a girl with a pale face and a long neck, which made her look like a lily, raised crescents of spiked eyelashes in insolent enquiry, but the lily was too busy shoveling down steak and kidney pie to watch for long. The other lunchers looked out casually too, and then went on lining themselves with soup and hors-d'oeuvres. In a dais beneath a droop of palms, Oliver Ogilvie's Ohio Octette began to drool out "I Kiss Your Little Hand, Madame."

"That's the third of those disgraceful processions I've seen this week," the first businessman said.

"You're right, Arthur: sheer damned lazy, that's what they are," the second man said.

"What beats me is why the fools can't understand that it's simply a question of economics and that employers can't afford to pay workers for doing nothing," the third man said.

"They ought to turn a machine-gun on the swine," the fourth man said. "Waiter, another four same agains."

"Tell me, Father," Elvira said across the table to the canon. "There's something very wrong with this country, isn't there?"

"With the whole world, I'm afraid, my dear," the canon said.

XXIV

IN THE HALL of Audiences, the squat, dumpy figure of His Holiness Pope Pius XI, two hundred and sixty-first Vicar of Christ on earth, passed among the pilgrims, scattering benedictions. Jammed in between three nuns from Montevideo and a baritone from Alaska, Monsignor O'Duffy murmured to his companions, Canon Smith and Canon Bonnyboat, "His Holiness and me have met before, so mind and let me dae the blethering." But the Supreme Pontiff's eyes were vacant behind his gleaming glasses as he passed the kneeling monsignor. He stretched out his hand, however, for Canon Smith to kiss his ring. "Vous êtes de quelle nationalité, mon fils?" he asked in French. "I am Scots, Holiness," Canon Smith replied in English, for he knew that the pope was an excellent linguist. "Ah, Sgotz," His Holiness murmured in the same tongue. "How ver-y int-er-esting." The two hundred and sixty-first Vicar of Christ passed on, scattering benedictions.

XXV

POOR MOTHER LECLERC died of a bloody flux on the Feast of Saint Francis Xavier, 1935, and was buried two days later in the convent garden, where Mother de la Tour had chosen her grave in a corner where all her loveliest flowers would bloom the next spring. Canon Bonnyboat sang the High Mass of Requiem, because he was supposed to be her especial friend, since it was he who had given the nuns the parrot; and the parrot himself, in a cage all covered with bows of black ribbon, was in the organ loft, because Reverend Mother knew that her lately departed daughter in Christ would have wished it so.

The bishop himself preached the panegyric. His voice was becoming feeble and wavering, because he was now seventy-five years of age, but he spoke out as loudly and as clearly as he could, because he wanted everyone to hear how beautiful he thought a nun's life was.

Monks and nuns, the bishop said, asked for no praise from the world for what they did; all they wanted was to be left alone to live their lives hid with God in Christ. "Be still and know that I am God." That was the command that each religious heard whispered in his heart, and it was the highest mission that any human soul could receive, for it was the only way to pierce through to the luster and the glory that shone forth on the other side of the curtain and to reflect a tiny shimmer of it back to the unheeding multitudes. It was the command that men and women needed most to obey today, when everything in the world was so noisy, from wireless sets to motor cars. It was the command that Mother Leclerc had heard in the France of her youth, when her hair had been black and strong and young, and her obedience had led her into strange places, but her eyes when she died had been, oh, so blue, because all her life she had been in love with Almighty God. When the bishop had said this, the parrot cawed out "per omnia saecula saeculorurn," but nobody laughed, because they were all so sorry that Mother Leclerc had left them.

The sober voices of the children in Mother Leclerc's class sang the offertory. They were only ten years of age, and one day they would forget all about Mother Leclerc and would walk with their lovers beside rivers and have children and grow old in strange beds, but they sang with sorrow: "Domine Jesu Christe, Rex gloriae, libera animas omnium fidelium defunctorum de poenis inferni, et de profundo lacu." As they sang, Canon Smith prayed for the repose of Mother Leclerc's soul. Then he prayed for the old sailor whom he had shriven so many long years ago and for Angus McNab and for Annie Rooney and for the boozy major and for D. H. Lawrence, who had known so much and who had known so little, that God might receive them, too, into everlasting dwellings. Then he prayed for the Abyssinians who were being killed by the Italians, that God might cradle their savage passing and make them quickly happy in Paradise; and for the Italians, too, he prayed, because death was sore for them as well as they lay with split faces and gouged eyes, and they, too, had once been little boys within walls. When he had finished praying, the children had got to "Fac eas, Domine, de morte transire ad vitam," and their voices had never faltered once, although they had loved Mother Leclerc so much.

When the Mass was over and the absolutions given, they carried the wooden box out into the garden and laid it in the hole beneath the leafless trees; and they all held lighted candles in their hands as a sign that Mother Leclerc's soul had not gone out but was shining somewhere still. Wrapped in his black-and-silver vestments, the frail old bishop prayed that God might grant eternal rest unto her and that perpetual light might shine upon her and that she might repose in peace.

When the service was over, Reverend Mother accompanied the bishop and Canon Smith to the gate of the convent, for the bishop had promised to give the canon a lift home in his car. "Elle était toujours si gaie, la pauvre, mais maintenant elle est probablement en train de chercher une bonne histoire pour raconter au Bon Dieu," she said.

The bishop wasn't at all sure that they gave the souls in Purgatory time to think up funny stories to tell God, but as the theologians had laid nothing down in the matter, and as he didn't want to hurt Reverend Mother's feelings, he kept his doubts to himself.

It was so long since he had been alone with the bishop that Canon Smith didn't know quite what to say to him as they trundled along deep ravines of ugly streets in his lordship's tiny tin truck. They knew each other well, of course, but not sufficiently well not to have to make noises at each other when they were alone together. Moreover, their natural shyness was increased by the fact that Canon Smith suspected that the bishop had always slightly disapproved of him since he had made that speech of his at his first chapter meeting and by the other fact that the bishop suspected his suspicion. The bishop, however, was the first to break their slightly awkward silence.

"I've been thinking lately about Father Scott," he said. "I've been wondering whether I oughtn't to move him on to another parish."

"The Church of the Holy Name will miss him terribly if you do," Canon Smith said. "In my opinion, he's the finest preacher we've had for years. It'll be an ungrateful task for one so awkwardly articulate as myself to preach at Benediction when he's gone."

"It's of the young man's own good that I'm thinking, and indeed of the ultimate good of the diocese as a whole," the bishop said. "If there's one thing more calculated to fan the flame of human vanity than being a popular actor, it's being a popular preacher. All these queues outside your church on Sunday evenings. And not only Catholics, either, but Protestants as well. A young man requires to be a saint indeed not to let that sort of success go to his head. And then some of the things that he says are rather startling. For instance, that remark of his about morality being something more positive than glamour girls refraining from uncovering their vaccination marks in the presence of archbishops. And then his statement about it being a matter of ecclesiastical discipline and not of divine law that priests in the diocese of Quebec should wear cassocks when they went swimming."

Canon Smith was relieved. He had been afraid that the bishop had been going to quote an even more startling phrase from Father Scott's address to the Men's Guild in the church hall on the Vigil of Saint John the Baptist for which he himself had taken the young man to task.

"I do not think, my lord, that Father Scott meant any harm by the statements you quote, and, what is more, I do not think he did any harm," he said. "And certainly he intended no disrespect to His Holiness's well-known views on women's dress, nor did he intend to criticize the rules and regulations prescribed by the Ordinary of

Quebec. All he meant was, I am sure, that ladies who wore long sleeves when they went to the Vatican and priests who dived off springboards in their cassocks would not because of their reticences alone enter into the Kingdom of Heaven." Behind his earnestness, he smiled as he remembered the day sixteen years ago when he himself had told the bishop how much purer he thought the world would be if women wore no clothes at all. "Father Scott has often told me that he thought the old truths wanted restating in language the people could understand. And indeed I think so myself. The Church possesses the truth, so why should she not shout out the sharp, uncompromising gospel of Christ in sharp, uncompromising language? As it is a greater sin before God for a duchess to underpay her footman than to appear before a cardinal showing a not very seductive sirloin of arm, why not say so? And Father Scott doesn't only preach Christianity, he acts it. Last month, for instance, when taking the last sacraments to a dying woman down by the docks, he found another woman in the same house keeping her two children out of bed because she was letting out their room to passing immoral couples. Father Scott told her exactly what he thought of her and himself turned the couple then in possession of the children's bedroom out into the street. You may say that such actions do not come within the normal scope of a priest's duties, but with all respect, I maintain that they ought to. I maintain that our Lord would have done exactly the same thing, because He, too, could lose His temper when the occasion demanded, as when He threw the money-changers out of the temple. I maintain, too, that if more priests acted and talked like Father Scott, many more people in the world would be Christians who are pagans now, and those who are already Christians would be better Christians. Doctrine, yes, the Blessed Sacrament and Heaven and Hell and Purgatory, but let us shout them out bravely and in new, loud words, so that the tired, old world of habit and respectability may hear and understand that Christianity is the only true and daring revolution."

"Probably we are both a little right and probably we are both a little wrong," the bishop said with a smile. "You know, each time that I walk behind a processional cross, I think I have a clearer view of our Lord's purposes. For sometimes the acolyte holds the cross straight and firm and erect, and sometimes he lets it slip so that it wobbles in his grasp. Well, the Christian religion's just like that, Canon: sometimes the battle's with us and our banners go forward; and sometimes the struggle's against us and our standards are tilted and torn; but always the grace of God is in our chrism, because He Himself poured it there."

The bishop said no more, but from his manner when they parted at the door of the presbytery, the canon understood that there was no immediate likelihood of Father Scott being moved to another parish.

On the other side of the street, Signor Sarno was walking with Father Scott himself, who had not been able to attend Mother Leclerc's funeral because he had had to stay at home in order to officiate at another funeral in the church. Canon Smith watched them from the window pacing up and down in front of a multi-colored poster that said something about "gorgeous girls and their playboy pals." It was obvious from the way that they stopped from time to time to wave their arms violently that they were having an argument. Then suddenly, they took off their hats at each other and shook hands. Signor Sarno thoughtfully ascended the steps of the cinema, and Father Scott came back across the road to the presbytery.

"I've just been giving old Sarno the works about Mr. B. Mussolini," the young priest said as he came in. "I told him that it was neither glorious, valorous, noble, nor epic for a great nation like Italy to bomb, gas, blister, blast, and massacre a horde of untrained and comparatively innocent peoples. At first he was inclined to protest, but I think I've gone a long way toward convincing him. And you'll never guess the advertisement I read in the *Catholic Trumpet* yesterday: 'Devonshire priest wants to purchase second-hand Bulgarian dictionary.' Now what the heck does a priest of God mean by wasting his time learning Bulgarian when there's as much downright wickedness in the world as there is today?"

"Perhaps the poor man wants to conquer downright wickedness in Bulgaria," said Canon Smith.

"Says you," said Father Scott.

XXVI

THE BISHOP ARRIVED five minutes late at the pro-cathedral on the Feast of Saint Philip and Saint James, 1937, when he was due to sing pontifical High Mass on the occasion of his sacerdotal golden jubilee. Canon Bonnyboat, however, who was to be master of ceremonies, was glad of the delay, because it gave him more time to decide who was to genuflect to whom and when and who were merely to remove their birettas, as six other bishops were to be in the choir and a host of abbots and priors as well, and even Doctor Adrian Fortescue, in *The Ceremonies of the Roman Rite Described*, seemed to have neglected to provide for such a beanfeast. Canon Smith, too, was slightly late, because he had been giving instructions to the architect about the new stone nave of the Holy Name, which the workmen were now building away at breakneck speed over the old tin nave, and he had to write and thank Elvira, who had sent him another five thousand pounds from America; but he arrived before the bishop all the same.

There was such a jam of ecclesiastics in the sacristy that there wasn't room for them all, even standing up, and the Franciscans from Kincairns had to sit on the dresser, but Canon Bonnyboat told them not to swing their legs so as not to spoil the varnish. The other bishops and abbots and priors stood round the bishop and smiled at him as he was helped into his red silk stockings and satin shoes, and the bishop told them that they had no idea how badly he sang High Mass these days, not at all like when he had been a young bishop of sixty, so he said. Then they all lined up in procession, with the acolytes first and then the priests and then the priors and then the abbots and then the bishops in their purple, and the bishop himself last of all with his master of ceremonies and assistants in their vestments; and Canon Bonnyboat said that none of the other bishops must give any blessings as they processed round the cathedral, but only the bishop, because it was he who was pontificating.

Canon Smith's eyes filled with tears as the organ roared out the "Ecce Sacerdos Magnus" and they entered the packed cathedral. What nonsense the left-wing intellectuals talked, he thought, when they spoke of "the phenomenon of our empty churches." Whatever churches were empty in Britain, the Catholic churches were always full. At four Masses each Sunday, the Holy Name was crammed from sanctuary rail to organ loft, and at some of the six Masses at the cathedral, people were standing bareheaded on the porch. And today the cathedral was crowded as it hadn't been since his lordship's consecration nearly forty years ago. The lord provost himself was there, and the lord lieutenant of the county and the chief constable and a major-general who had come all the way from Scottish Command Headquarters; and behind and around those distinguished, pop-eyed, glossy heretics come out to do honor to the bishop swarmed the great, familiar family of God's faithful: from the high-class Lady Ippecacuanha, with a missal the size of an encyclopedia, and the nuns all twittering with excitement, to the knobbly, old charwomen and their grubby brats and the splodges of babies yelping in their mothers' arms at the back of the church near the holy-water stoups.

Father Scott preached the sermon, because he was the best preacher in the diocese, but first he knelt before the bishop for his blessing. Then Father Scott stood up in the pulpit and said, "In the Name of the Father, and of the Son, and of the Holy Ghost," just like that, and the babies at the back stopped their yowling and the bishops in their purple and the abbots and priors in their habits and the canons and the plain, big-eared parish priests all listened mightily, because they had heard what a very fine preacher he was; and behind a pillar, in her humble, square, old coat, his mother squeezed his father's hand, because it was their own son who was going to preach before all these holy men.

They were celebrating that day the fiftieth anniversary of their bishop's ordination to the priesthood, Father Scott said, and on such occasions it was customary to preach happy, safe sermons about the wonders wrought in human souls by the operation of sacramental grace. Well, he wasn't going to preach a happy, safe sermon, because the world in which they lived was not a happy, safe world; instead, he was going to preach what some people might call an explosive sermon, nor was he going to apologize for it, because if Christianity was anything, it was an explosive idea, just as all the sacraments that the bishop had administered in the fifty years of his priesthood might be said to be explosive sacraments, since the center of them all had been the Holy Ghost, Who was a dynamite that blasted away sin.

In olden days, the reason for most of the world's miseries had been that Christians proclaimed with their lips and dissembled in their hearts; today, Christians didn't bother even to proclaim with their lips, and, although some people might laud this omission as sincerity, he thought that it was a bad sign, since it indicated that there were no longer enough true Christians in the world to exact from the less virtuous a hypocrisy that was, in its twisted way, a compliment. Even Catholics, to whom knowledge of the truth had been granted, quickly forgot in the marketplace what they had learned from the pulpit and aped the manners and the methods of those who claimed that this world was all. This defection of Catholics as a whole could not be denied, for they numbered about a fifth of the world's total population; and if their practice had equaled their faith, the history of the last nineteen years must surely have been different.

For what had they got to show for the more than six thousand days they had lived since the eleventh of November, 1918, when peace for all time had been promised to the world? What except that they could now fly across the Atlantic instead of sail across it, that cinemas now talked, and that on the wireless the music went round and round so that by merely pushing a button one could have Bach for breakfast and "You're My Sweetie Pie" for tea? But that sort of thing was not progress; on the contrary, it was the reverse of progress, for the superabundance of mechanical diversions stunted men's souls, because they demanded no effort from their imagination. This would have been bad enough even in their fathers' time, when men's occupations stimulated their intellects, but in these days, when the subdivision of labor had made most tasks dull, it was almost disastrous.

The causes of these miseries were numerous. Firstly, there was the almost universal agnosticism that came not from the intellect but from the heart, which was glad to be able to disbelieve because sin now appeared to be without consequence. Secondly, there was the theory that the sole purpose of education was to teach men to earn their livings, whereas its real purpose was to teach them to love God and humanity, both of whom manifested themselves more clearly outside laboratories and counting-houses than inside them. Thirdly, there was the general decline in honesty and high purposefulness and, as a result of the literature of disillusion, the conviction that nobody else practiced honesty and high purposefulness either. For we were all, in the dreadful phrase of the American cinema, "wise guys" these days and no longer believed that anybody in the whole world acted from disinterested motives but that everybody had an axe to grind. The test of any project was now purely practical: whether it would work; business was business, so the city men said, which was another way of saying that they could swindle in the name of commerce. Money was as money did, they cried, calling up from the grave the ghost of George Adam Smith, and political economy was a normative science, they said, that aimed at showing how men tended to behave in certain circumstances and not how they ought to behave. Well, the Church of God was not a normative Church but a thundering, teaching, shouting, preaching Church, crying out to men what they must do if they were to be saved, and he as a priest of that Church had no hesitation in saying that the political economists were talking through their hats and that money was not as money did but rather the measure of man's inability to obey Almighty God and love his neighbor as himself.

Fourthly and finally, there was the myth of progress that assumed that men went on becoming automatically and inevitably more and more civilized and that the habits of tomorrow would be as superior to those of today as those of today were to those of yesterday. This, too, was a grave error. Moving forward in time did not necessarily mean moving forward in ethics. The citizen of London today was not, because he read the *News of the World* on Sunday afternoons, superior to the fourth-century-before-Christ citizen of Athens who went to see a performance of Aeschylus's *Agamemnon*. The young lady who was popular with the men at dances because she had no body odor was not an improvement on Saint Elizabeth of Hungary, who must have smelled quite a lot after succoring her lepers, unless, which was unlikely, the young lady happened to think a better kind of thought than Saint Elizabeth of Hungary. For true progress was moral rather than mechanical: if there were to be more switches, more buttons, more batteries, there must also be more restraints, more austerities, more unselfishness, more humilities, more prayers, more contemplations on the real end of man.

The world was in its present agony because men had not been willing to understand that the lamp of western civilization, which had been lighted by the Catholic Church, had to be tended constantly or it would go out forever. God's housekeeping had to be done every day afresh, or moth and rust would corrupt the fabric and the furniture wrought by patient men through the centuries. It was because men had refused to do God's chores that the peace of the world was again threatened, as was evidenced by the dreadful civil war at that moment raging in Spain.

Watching the bishop blessing the incense through the intercession of Blessed Michael the Archangel, Canon Smith wondered how he had taken Father Scott's sermon; but it was not until they were back in the sacristy and the bishop called him over that he knew.

"Well, Canon, I am afraid that I shall have to move that young man of yours after all," he said.

"But, my lord, what he said wasn't wrong," Canon Smith protested.

"It is because what he said was so right that I'll have to move him," the bishop said. "I am going to make him rector of Our Lady, Mirror of Justice, Gormnevis. Some of the canons won't like it, but they'll just have to lump it, I'm afraid."

XXVII

WHEN HE WENT to say his prayers in the High Kirk on the Feast of Saint Andrew, 1938, Canon Smith knew that he wouldn't meet his old friend the minister, because the minister was dead; instead, on the porch there was a grand, new notice about the young folks' weekday evening service that said in big letters "Come and Bring a Chum," because the new minister was very modern and believed in youth. Some of the youth he believed in were standing on the steps when Canon Smith arrived, saying that they thought they'd better sort of attend choir practice next week as the new minister kind of liked it, and instead of saying "cheerio" when they took farewell of one another, they said, "cheery-bye," because that was the fashion these days, and even, in certain parts of the diocese, "cheery-ta-ta" as well.

Kneeling in his accustomed place, the canon prayed quietly and earnestly for the world, which seemed to be going from bad to worse. He prayed especially for the great cartloads of dead constantly appearing before Almighty God for judgment from the Spanish civil and from the Sino-Japanese wars, that Christ might grant a special balm to souls so rudely torn from their bodies. He prayed for the old sailor and the boozy major and Angus McNab and Annie Rooney in case they were still in Purgatory, and he prayed that they would pray for him if they were already in Heaven and making holy whoopee with the saints. Then he prayed for God's erring children in Christ, Adolf and Benito, because they had both been baptized and confirmed and so ought to have known so very much better than to rant and rave and threaten the world. Then he prayed for the bishop, that he might still continue to govern wisely, and for Father Scott, that God might temper his tongue and still give him courage, and for Elvira in America, that she might abound in grace, and for his old pals Monsignor O'Duffy and Canon Bonnyboat, and for himself, too, that God might soften their ending years. Then he went out onto the porch, where he found Sir Dugald Ippecacuanha practicing mashie shots with his walking-stick.

"Afternoon, padre," Sir Dugald greeted, and added that he was surprised to meet the priest in such a locality.

Canon Smith explained his practice and the reason for it, and Sir Dugald said that it was a pity that more clergymen weren't as broadminded as he, and the canon said that he wasn't broadminded at all and that, to be quite frank, he was glad he wasn't, because broadmindedness was often another name for shallow thinking. This made Sir Dugald pop his poached eyes a bit, but, being a polite heretic, he quickly changed the subject and asked Canon Smith how the building of his new nave was progressing.

"Not at all badly, thank you," the canon answered. "Indeed, it should be finished and the church ready for consecration in a year from now if there isn't war."

"War, of course there won't be war," Sir Dugald said fiercely. "Why should there be war? Didn't Hitler say that Czechoslovakia was the last territorial demand that he had to make in Europe? Of course, there's the question of colonies, but with a little goodwill on both sides, even that shouldn't prove too difficult. And then that agreement Chamberlain brought back with him from Munich. Peace in our time, he said it meant. And then those conversations he's going to have with Old Musso. Of course, I know the warmongers don't like Chamberlain, but I'm not a warmonger and never was. Indeed, I said as much in the House the other day. 'There is no earthly reason why two great countries like Britain and Germany shouldn't work together for the maintenance of peace and prosperity,' I said. 'Let us talk peace to Hitler and we shall have peace.' And between you and me and the doorpost, I'm beginning to think that the last war was a hideous mistake. Great Britain and Germany ought to have got together years ago. Of course, I know that the Germans are cruel, and there's that business about the Jews and all that, but after all, we're not angels ourselves, so why make such a racket about what doesn't concern us?"

"But it does concern us, Sir Dugald," the canon said. "It concerns us because it concerns Almighty God, Who wishes us to extend our charity even to those we have never seen and shall never see. It's merely a matter of exercising the imagination, that's all: thinking of their hair and ears and eyes, thinking of them in the tender loneliness of sleep. If we do that, we can no longer hate. And if there's one thing more terrible than war, it's the kind of peace we've been having for the last twenty years: even death and destruction and mangled human bodies couldn't stench more pungently to Heaven than all those beastly advertisements about depilatories and toothpastes and children's bowels. And I don't trust Hitler one little bit, and I consider that Mussolini is a big, blustering baboon."

"Canon, Canon, you surprise me," Sir Dugald said.

"Indeed, Sir Dugald, there are times when I surprise myself," Canon Smith said.

XXVIII

WAR HAD COME to Britain again, the sailors were lurching out of the public houses again, and the tough women were lurching with them, only they no longer wore high laced boots, because the rubrics had changed in these matters.

War had come again to the parish of the Holy Name also. Canon Smith no longer had a curate to say his early Masses for him, and on Sundays he had both Masses to say or sing himself and to preach two sermons as well, so that it was quite like old times again, except that he was now seventy-one years of age and much more creaky at genuflecting than he used to be.

War had come to the building trade too, so that it was almost impossible to get any masons to complete the now nearly finished new nave; but Canon Bonnyboat, who had hobnobbed quite a lot with the Benedictines at Buckfast on his highbrow, liturgical holidays, said that the monks had taught him quite a lot about church building and that he would be more than pleased to place his knowledge at the service of Canon Smith and show him how, with the aid of a few staunch friends, he could polish off the remainder of the church himself. So on three afternoons a week, Canon Smith and Canon Bonnyboat and Monsignor O'Duffy and Father Scott humphed and plastered and smeared and tapped and felt happy sitting across high stones in the sky. Generally, the bishop came along as well, but he said that heights always made him feel giddy, so he stayed on the ground and mixed the mortar and pushed it about on a wheelbarrow.

It was cold work in March, 1940, sitting up aloft with the wind blowing about ears, but Monsignor O'Duffy said that any discomfort that they might be experiencing ought to be more than counterbalanced by the knowledge that they were really and truly doing Almighty God's handiwork, and that in his opinion wars would cease forever if men all over the world could be given the high and sweet privilege of tiring their arms and legs and eyes by hewing, smiting, carving, and carrying for God and His saints. He felt so happy as he said this that he said he simply must sing aloud, so with his hat on the back of his head, he bawled a song that he said had been very popular in the music-halls in the nineties:

"No more getting up at half-past six,
Climbing up a ladder with a hodful of bricks;
No more clay pipes, nothing but cigars,
For now I am a driver on the tramway cars."

Canon Bonnyboat said at once that he didn't think that the bishop would approve of a priest singing a song like that in the open air, so the monsignor, looking down to the little splodge of bishop below busy with his wheelbarrow, hastily roared "Per omnia saecula saeculorum" as loudly as he could.

"I sometimes feel that this war might have been prevented if myself and others had not kept silent from notions of human respect on matters on which we felt deeply," Canon Smith said. "If only we had preached more boldly that Christianity is not a respectable habit of restraint but a loud, vulgar, clamorous heroism."

"You can say what you like, but in my mind, there is no doubt at all," Canon Bonnyboat said. "This war is a crusade."

"I must confess that I am coming to be rather wearied by the phrase," Father Scott said. "Indeed, the whole phraseology of wartime rhetoric strikes me as boring, inaccurate, and very often insincere."

"That's because nothing ever sounds quite so dreadful as the right phrase on the wrong lips," Canon Bonnyboat said. "But the fact remains that whether we like or not the accents and the faces of some of the people who are fighting with us, our cause remains just."

"All the same, I can't help wishing that the politicians would give up taking us for a set of complete nincompoops," Father Scott said. "They speak of the present conflict as 'the birth pangs of a new Europe.' The metaphor is inexact. In birth, a mother either recovers or dies, and if the former, she herself experiences the joy of possessing her child; whereas in this bloody battle, thousands will be maimed in loneliness, and the new Europe they have brought forth will probably be eaten up by the fat swine who stayed at home and made money and smoked cigars. And all this cant about fighting for freedom. Is the coal-miner free? Is the laborer free? Is not all freedom dependent upon economic circumstances? And again, isn't there a virtue in obedience?"

"And I must say that I wish some of our apostles of liberty could walk more humbly and righteously," Canon Smith said as he looked down on the hordes swarming into Signor Sarno's cinema to see Spencer Tracey.

"What a lot of clavering blethers you all are to be sure," Monsignor O'Duffy said. "The world's Almighty God's broth, so perhaps ye'd better let Him stir it and boil it His own way."

None of the priests minded the monsignor speaking like that, because they knew that deep down behind his purple stock, he was just as worried about the war as they were and knew that patriotism wasn't enough. Below them, far away out along the bend of the railway line, at the junction of the golf course and Sir Dugald Ippecacuanha's estate, a puff of smoke appeared above the trees, and a miniature worm of train rolled tinily along the embankment. In the pattern of their garden, the nuns were walking, with their hands folded, up and down past Mother de la Tour's flowers no longer, because she too had died and had been buried beside Mother Leclerc. And on the surface of the sea, the wind played, ruffling it like a girl's frock. Looking down at the great, stamped-out peace of Scotland, Canon Smith was reassured.

"Perhaps we're too impatient," he thought.

When they finished their work and climbed down to the ground again, they found Sir Dugald Ippecacuanha laying off the bishop, who was washing the mortar off his hands.

"Of course, I've always said all along that Chamberlain ought to go," Sir Dugald was saying. "And between you and me, your lordship, I was one of the few who wanted to take a strong stand at Munich. And that fellow Baldwin. The way he led us all up the garden. Only he didn't lead me, I'm glad to say. I knew Germany too well to be taken in. 'Beware of Germany,' I used to say. If Churchill and Eden and Duff Cooper and I pointed out to the house once, we pointed out a hundred times. No, sir. With all respect to your cloth, as far as I'm concerned, the only good German's a dead German."

As they stood and listened, Canon Smith and Father Scott saw with dismay that Sir Dugald really believed what he was saying.

XXIX

WHEN HE ARRIVED at the pro-cathedral for Monsignor O'Duffy's funeral, the bishop was driven in in his car by his master of ceremonies, who had to do a quick change afterward; but the bishop himself had no quick changing to do, because he came in his purple silk and his lace through the streets quite openly, and even Protestants took off their hats to him as he passed because he was too old for anybody to hate any longer, and even the Congregationalist official had made no difficulty about giving him extra coupons for his petrol.

There was such a cram in the church that the procession had almost to fight its way to the high altar: the Franciscans were there, the Jesuits were there, the Dominicans were there, the Benedictines were there, the Helpers of the Holy Souls were there, the nuns from the convent were there, the lord provost and members of the town council were there, the management and team of the Shamrock Football Club were there, the Episcopal Dean and the ministers of all the Protestant churches were there, the Salvation Army was there, the Saint Patrick Cooperative Society was there, the Plumbers' and Gasfitters' Trade Union was there, the chorus girls from the revue at the Duke of York's Theater were there, the chartered accountants were there, the lawyers were there, the bank managers were there, the town territorials were there, the university professors were there, the tram drivers, the stokers, the chimney sweeps, the schoolchildren, the babies he had baptized, and the harlots he had rebuked in the street were there, all surging in a steaming soup because a great and a good and a humble and a simple man had been called away by Almighty God.

Canon Smith sang the Mass of Requiem, because he had been the monsignor's oldest friend, and Canon Bonnyboat was deacon and Canon Muldoon was subdeacon. As he stood at the right-hand side of the altar to sing the collect, the sob in his heart was so great that it burst right through into his voice; but even as he faltered, the echo of tones that had been used to him at that very altar came back to him: "Sing oot louder, Tam; the auld wives at the back'll no be able tae hear ye"; so he mastered his gulp and sang out with all his might that God's holy angels might take Patrick Ignatius O'Duffy and lead him to the home of Paradise.

When the service was over, the coffin was carried from the church on the shoulders of the Shamrock Football Team, whom the monsignor had used to encourage from the grandstand with both fingers in his mouth. Right through the crowd on the steps, the shining coffin was passed and was laid in the hearse, which was to be driven by James Finnegan, who had once knocked Battling Sambo out of the ring in the presence of King Edward VII. Immediately behind the hearse, the pipe band of the Territorials formed up, with the drum major enormous in his kilt and a smasher of a moustache that looked like two Persian cats' tails. Then came the members of the town council in their cocked hats and robes, preceded by their mace-bearer. Then came the principal and senate of the University in their gowns and robes, only their files weren't quite even, as the Reader in Icelandic Philology got mixed up with Miss Zizi Ashton, leading lady in the *Gay Girls* revue, whose place in the procession came immediately afterward. Then came the chartered accountants, the lawyers, and the stockbrokers, sorry dogs most of them, and the bank managers with mincing mien. Then came the plumbers and the gasfitters and the stokers and the tram drivers, humble and knobby men who tinkered at dull tasks to the greater glory of God. Then came the clergy of other denominations in their ordinary clothes without their robes, because it was as individuals to an individual they were paying their last respects. Then came the nuns stretching like great black-and-white birds on the cover of a book by Anatole France. In front of the coffin went the priests in their cottas and cassocks, the canons in their fur and their purple, the friars in their brown and their black and their white, the monks in their cowls, the acolytes trying to keep their candles lighted in the wind, and last of all the bishop and his assistants in their stiff black-and-gold. And behind all came the great surge of God's great, humble, holy unwashed, weeping and sniveling and snottering in their shawls because they would never again hear the voice of Patrick Ignatius O'Duffy telling them that they would burn like kindling if they didn't come to Mass on Sundays.

Through the advertisements for Pepsodent and Guinness and Players and Mine's A Minor the procession passed, but it wasn't only through them, because the streets were so blocked with other mourners that all the tramways had had to be stopped. For the most part, it was the poor who had come out to see Monsignor O'Duffy go by for the last time, but some of the eleven-o'clock coffee-drinking women were there as well, caught in the crowd between changing their library books and buying liver salts, popping their silly little eyes at a popularity they were too imbecile to understand. But the poor understood all right, and the ragged children sat on their parents' shoulders, and those who were big enough clambered up the lampposts. If the monsignor had been alive, they would have cheered, but as he was dead, they wept instead, and those who weren't weeping had a great distress on their faces because they knew that a great, clumsy slice of man who had known all about God's mercy would walk among them no more. And nobody thought at all about it being illegal in Scotland for priests to process in public in their vestments, and so the poetry of Christ's Church went by, casting a fleeting reflection of meaning upon the sprawl of the city.

Past Signor Sarno's cinema house bawling out about Hedy Lamarr, past the Episcopal cathedral where God wore a blazer, past the steps of the Carlton-Elite with the angels of men ascending and descending, past the theosophical library with its spread of Mrs. Annie Besant, past the new subterranean lavatory for gentlemen, past the bowling green where the monsignor had shown his multi-colored shirtsleeves on summer Wednesday evenings, past the windows of the Conservative Club packed with faces that ruled the world, past the Duke of York's Theater, past the Port Said Dancing Club where the hostesses in their vapors flung fish and chips at one another, past the new, red-brick Congregational Church, on, on, on, out into the grand, green splash of the country.

When at length they reached the cemetery, the acolytes all had to light their candles again, as the flames had long since gone out. The bishop blessed the grave with incense and with holy water and prayed that the soul of Patrick Ignatius O'Duffy might be joined to the angelic choir; and with the cold trees all about them, the clergy and the laity all blubbered like bairns because a holy, humble, yelling, blundering, delicate priest had been gathered by God.

XXX

ON THE EVE of the Feast of Saint Ephrem the Syrian, deacon, confessor, and Doctor of the Church, 1940, when Canon Smith went to the convent to hear the nuns' confessions and say his Office beneath the trees, there were still more people walking, grown up, about the streets whom he didn't know, but he knew Signor Sarno all right, swinging out from his cinema in his Local Defense Volunteer uniform with a glengarry cocked over one Neapolitan eye, just as though he had been born in Pittenweem. The bills over the cinema were now saying something about a man called Tyrone Power, but there was also another bill, almost as big, which said: "This Cinema is British-Owned."

"Buon giorno, reverendo padre mio," Signor Sarno greeted. "E come sta per questo bel tempo? Reverendo Father, you were right, but so right. That Mussolini is a scoundrel, an oh, so blown-out bladder of conceit. And to attack poor France at such a momento. Reverendo Father, it make my Scottish blood boil but terribly, for I am Pritish now, reverendo Father, and willingly will I give my unworthy life in defense of democracy and freedom, and the ponny purple heather. And Elvira, she think the same as I do, for she send me in a letter from America to say that she is going to make no more pictures, but is coming home to fight for truth with the valorous and courageous women of the A.T.S., though what it stands for ho completamente dimenticato."

When he had heard the nuns' confessions, the canon walked among Mother de la Tour's flowers, because Reverend Mother had given him permission to say his Office there. Up and down he paced, with the trees throwing lovely shadows on the red and black Latin words in his breviary. "Excelsus super omnes gentes Dominus: et super coelos gloria eius." The canon felt guilty at being able to say such beautiful words in a summer garden when so many young men were at that very moment dying so painfully in France. As he thanked God for his good fortune, Reverend Mother came across the grass to talk to him. The canon could see from her eyes that she had been weeping about France, so he began to speak of something else.

"I passed on my way here two undertakers' assistants marching along the pavements with their agnostic bowler hats banged well down over their ears, and I thought how dreadful it was that even Catholics should give their dead to the care of such ghouls," he said. "It has long been my opinion that the dead should be laved, shrouded, and carried to the earth by those who have known their bodies for a long time and have, through association and affection, come to realize that they are indeed the temple of the Holy Ghost; but failing that, they should be handed over to be tended by a religious order whose members would reverently perform the last tidying, since they would know that the body of even a wicked man is holy when it is dead, because it is the shadow of a soul terribly at Christ's mercy. And then even the saints, as Cardinal Manning said, were once as we were, with hands and feet and ears and eyes. Reverend Mother, you are not listening," he said.

"Je pense à mon pauvre pays, si terriblement meutri," Reverend Mother said. "Oh, I know well that France has sinned, that she has had great lusts and great passions, but at least they were *great* lusts and *great* passions. And I know that she has persecuted the Church and driven out the monks and nuns, but at least that showed that she was not indifferent to religion, and hatred can so often be lighted into love. And then think of all the saints who have trodden her roads and loved Almighty God beneath her thatches. It is not just, monsieur le chanoine, it is not just."

"Canon Scott said a very wise thing the other day," Canon Smith said, "I know that some people think that it was a little unwise on the part of the bishop to have appointed so young a man administrator of the cathedral, but Canon Scott has shown many proofs of his wisdom. For one thing, he was fair about the Spanish civil war when most of the rest of us clergy were unfair. Well, he told me the other day that in his opinion, delayed action Holy Ghost was very much more dangerous than delayed action bombs. Indeed, he said that it was because of delayed action Holy Ghost that we have the delayed action bombs. In other words, we are reaping the rewards of putting off till an indefinite tomorrow the imperative duty of corresponding with God's grace. And even now that the indefinite tomorrow has become the definite today, we only *hear* the still, small voice."

"But Paris," Reverend Mother said. "To think of all those filthy boots in Paris! But surely, somewhere they will hold them. On the Loire, perhaps. Perhaps on the wireless there is news already that our fortunes have turned."

But Mother de la Tour's wireless when they went in to listen to it was inspiring the war for freedom, righteousness, truth, and democracy only by moaning:

"I love the sound of the chapel bells,
I love the dancing in the good hotels."

Canon Smith listened with a bitter expression, but Reverend Mother placed her hand behind her ear because she felt that some important news might come through at any moment. When at length it did and the impersonal voice announced that Marshal Pétain had asked the German High Command to make known on what terms they would be prepared to grant an armistice, she shut her eyes and stood up very straight.

"De profundis clamavi ad te, Domine," she said. "Canon, there is something I should very much like you to help me to do."

Half an hour later, when Canon Smith left the convent, the flag was flying from the gates at half-mast, only this time it wasn't the white flag of France but the tricolor.

XXXI

IN HIS PALACE, which was a semi-detached villa on John Knox Road, James Michael Gabriel, by the grace of God and the favor of the Apostolic See, Lord Bishop of the diocese, lay dying. He had been shriven and received Holy Communion. His tired, old hands and feet and ears and eyes and mouth and nose had been anointed with the holy oils that he himself had blessed in his own cathedral on Maundy Thursday. In a creaking voice, he had recited the Creed for the last time, confessing that he believed in the Holy Catholic Church, the forgiveness of sins, and the life everlasting. Around his bed, the canons knelt in their big boots while Canon Muldoon read aloud the prayers for the dying. The canons were all old men, too, now, with wrinkled, pouchy faces and scrubs of hair growing out of their ears, except Joseph Dominic Aloysius Canon Scott, of course, who was only thirty-three but a braw, bonny priestlet for all that. "In the name of angels and archangels, in the name of thrones and dominions; in the name of principalities and powers; in the name of virtues, cherubim and seraphim; in the name of patriarchs and prophets ..." As he listened to Canon Muldoon broguing out the Church's thunder, Canon Smith wondered how much longer it would be before they were saying the same words for him. Then, from the bed, the bishop whispered that he would like to bless them all before he died, and one by one the canons went forward and knelt under his hand.

"Ego te benedico in Nomine Patris, et Filii, et Spiritus Sancti," the bishop said to Canon Poustie. "Francis Xavier, go in peace." Canon Poustie's eyes were so blurred with tears that he nearly tripped over Canon Dobbie as he came back to his place, but Canon Dobbie quite understood because he was weeping too.

For most of them, too, he had a special message, as for Canon Bonnyboat, to whom he said: "Christopher, go in peace; perhaps I'll be better at keeping my miter on in the next world than in this, and thank you for putting me right so often." To Canon Muldoon, he said: "Go in peace, Aloysius Patrick Francis, and I hope the money comes in for that new organ." To Canon Sellar, he said: "Go in peace, James; I'm sorry I shan't be able to preside at your Forty Hours for you." To Canon Dobbie, he said: "Go in peace, Peter, and I hope the new brassie turns out all right." To Canon Smith, he said, just as though their argument about poetry had been yesterday and not thirty-three long, dusty, petroly, wrapped-up years ago: "Go in peace, Thomas Edmund. For the world to be safe, the young man has got to live his poetry as well as murmur it, and thank you for being so often right when I was wrong." But it was to Canon Scott that he spoke the most of all, laying his hand on the young man's shoulders after he had blessed him and telling him a lot of things that must have been very holy indeed, because he whispered them so low that nobody else could hear.

"Deus misericors, Deus clemens," Canon Muldoon began to pray again when the bishop had finished, but the bishop whispered that he wasn't quite ready to die yet and would like to say a few words to them all.

First of all, he asked their pardon for any harshnesses or injustices or incomprehensions of which he might have been guilty, saying that it wasn't easy to be a bishop sometimes, because although a bishop had the Holy Ghost to help him, he was still in most matters an ordinary man liable to err, because that had been God's way of building the Church, out of the rickety human planks and bits of odd wood He had found lying about the world.

Secondly, he commended to their care, their thought, and their charity the diocese that he had loved and ruled for more than thirty-five years. Especially did he enjoin upon them the duty of seeking heavenly guidance in the matter of choosing his successor, since his task would be hard in a world that did not seem to understand that it was at war solely because men and women had not been willing to go on practicing those reticences, moderations, and obediences out of which had grown their civilization.

Thirdly, he asked them to persevere in their own vocations. It was difficult sometimes, in face of the vast apathy of men, to feel that what one had said from the pulpit had been of much avail. When one thought of all the sermons that were preached every Sunday all over the world, and when one considered the bitterness and the hatred in men's hearts today, one was tempted to conclude that the Church of God had failed. But the Church of God had not failed, because God had promised that even the gates of Hell should not prevail against her, and besides, her mission was set in eternity and not in time. It was perhaps they who as preachers had failed and not the laity who as listeners had failed. Perhaps the truth had been too big for them and had ridden clumsily on their lips. He was sure that at least his old friend Canon Smith would know what he meant when he quoted a phrase he had once read in a book by a man named Thornton Wilder to the effect that rhetoric had ruined religion. Perhaps they had thought and expressed themselves too much in phrases, wrapping Christ's truth in verbal reach-me-downs instead of themselves cutting and tailoring individual, telling words.

Let him give them a secular instance. The first savage who had beaten out the phrase "as white as snow" had been both an original thinker and a poet, but thousands of millions of repetitions by the thoughtless of his simile had robbed it not only of beauty but of meaning as well. The same held true in sacred matters. The laity had grown so used to hearing certain phrases flung at them that they could sit and listen unmoved. Or, what was worse, the familiarity of the words, the monotony of the same concatenation of sounds, aroused in them an apathy to religion and deadened all desire to cooperate with sanctifying grace.

He was not going to ask them to become poets, because the perfect carving, molding, and ordering of words was a special gift from God and one, unfortunately, that was not granted with the laying-on of hands; but he was going to suggest that they should write their sermons word by word instead of phrase by phrase. He could give them no rules in the matter, but he would suggest that there were times when it was more telling to say "Church" instead of "our Holy Mother the Church," "mercy" instead of "everlasting mercy," "Lent" instead of "the penitential season of Lent," for adjectives could petrify as well as qualify nouns. Finally, he thanked them for having been such good priests, unobtrusively reflecting Christ's martyrdom in the austerity of their daily lives. He asked them to pray for him when he was dead, as he had no doubt at all that he was in for a good dose of Purgatory, as he had often been slothful and worldly in his unguarded moments.

"Deus misericors, Deus clemens," Canon Muldoon began to pray again, but before he got to the end of the prayer, the bishop was dead.

XXXII

THE BISHOP LEFT one hundred and seventy-eight pounds three shillings and fourpence when he died, and he left it all in trust to Canon Scott "to be used for the conversion of Scotland to the True Faith." Most of the canons felt that an even greater sum would be required to do the trick, but they placed Canon Scott's name at the head of the three names they sent to Rome, and the pope agreed that he should be the new bishop, even though he was only thirty-four years old, and everybody was very pleased because they knew that that had been the bishop's wish or otherwise he wouldn't have left the young man all that money.

The grubby-mouthed urchins for whom Monsignor O'Duffy had blown up balloons in 1927 were dying in Libya when the new bishop was consecrated in the pro-cathedral on the Feast of Saint Philip and Saint James, 1942, *coram* Lady Ippecacuanha in her green W.V.S. uniform. The bishop of Iona and the Lochs was the consecrating bishop, but Canon Smith's snooty cousin from England was a consecrator as well, because there had to be three consecrators to make sure that the Holy Ghost was properly handed on.

Afterward there was a grand luncheon at the Carlton-Elite, because even though it was wartime, it was not every day that a young man of thirty-four became a bishop. Old James Scott was at the high table, sandwiched in between the bishop of Iona and the Lochs and the snooty old bishop from England, only this time he didn't have to wear his tramway-man's uniform, because he had retired from points duty two years ago, and in any case, he would probably have been allowed the day off. Mrs. Scott was at the high table, too, but she hadn't been able to buy a new hat, because she hadn't known that her son was going to be made a bishop and had allowed her coupons to run out. There were also a number of Polish, French, and Czechoslovak officers in uniform, because the Church in the town was very international these days. Poor Canon Bonnyboat wasn't there, though, because he had had a stroke three months previously and was now living in the Aged and Infirm Priests' Home, which was especially unfortunate just then, as he could have prevented their lordships from making quite a lot of bloomers at the consecration. Elvira was there, however, very neat in the second subaltern's uniform, because she had given up filmmaking and had come home to join the A.T.S. Canon Smith sat beside her and he thought that she was looking lovelier than ever; she still said that she wasn't ever going to get married, but she said that she might become a nun when the war was over if she found out that she loved God enough.

The spam was excellent, and Canon Smith felt in fine fettle as he rose to propose the new bishop's health and to wish him *ad multos annos*. He began by saying that he thought that he had a special right to propose the toast, because he himself had baptized his lordship thirty-four years previously, and it wasn't every priest who could boast that he'd seen babies turn into bishops.

They needn't be afraid, however: he wasn't going to make a long speech, because he had no need to, as their new bishop's qualities were too well known to them all. All he was going to say was this: their old bishop had been a great and a wise ruler, and his chief concern had been that the diocese that he had loved so much should have a great and wise ruler when he died. That was the only sense in which ambition was lawful for a Christian: ambition for the work and not for self.

The true poet cared only that great poetry should be written and not that he himself should write it. So it was with priests. Good priests cared only that the flickering flame should be handed down the line of tapers and not that they themselves should be the tapers. Bishops were God's chosen tapers, the beacons that He had lighted with the Holy Ghost down the centuries and then passed the flame on to others. That understanding, he was sure, would be in their new bishop's mind as he processed down their churches in his purple and gold: the understanding that he himself would crumble back to dust but that God's glory that he carried would blaze on forever. He felt that there was something else that he ought to say, but he couldn't think of it, so he just wished the new bishop a long life and a happy one and then sat down.

"My dear Thomas, I had no idea that you were such an orator," his snooty cousin said as they stood in the cloakroom buttoning on their coats. "In fact, my dear fellow, you're wasted in these barbarous parts. You ought to have come to England: you'd have gone ever so much farther."

"It's the Church I want to go far," Canon Smith said, and then changed the subject, because, after all, it wasn't his business to snub the snooty bishop.

XXXIII

THE NEW BISHOP calculated that since the arrival of the Poles, the most popular of the mortal sins had increased in the diocese by 243.75 percent, and accordingly he had ordered that the Polish military chaplains should be given every opportunity for hearing confessions in all chapels and churches. Canon Smith was especially glad of this order, because he hadn't been sure that his new penitents understood his directives in French ever since the day when the newly absolved Polish major had said to him at the door of the church: "Mai girl friend is going to have a baby. It is very naice. And after the war mai waife she will be very pleased when I take the baby back to Poland and say: 'Look, Wanda, here is a present for you.'" Besides, the Polish priest was generally able to say the early Mass for him on Sundays, which was a great help with himself so old and young curates so hard to come by.

The Polish penitents were still stretching in rows outside Father Lidzowski's box as Canon Smith left his confessional on a Saturday afternoon in September, 1942. There were also a few files of French sailors ruled in lines of blue and white outside the French priest's confessional, for Général de Gaulle's military chaplain had come over from Dunoon because there was a Free French ship in. The canon gazed for a few minutes with pleasure at the spectacle of tough men kneeling and then went into the presbytery to take off his cassock, for he had promised to call on Canon Bonnyboat at the Aged and Infirm Priests' Home.

Outside the church, however, the tough men weren't kneeling as, along with girls in isosceles skirts, they muscled into the queue outside Signor Sarno's cinema, which was now advertising two ladies called Veronica Lake and Greer Garson. The admission to the stalls was now one-and-nine and to the balcony two-and-six, and the premises were more British owned than ever, because Signor Sarno was now a sergeant in the Home Guard and marched behind the pipes with a real Ecclefechan swing. But the signore wasn't standing on the steps as the canon passed; instead, when the priest called into the ice-cream shop to purchase his own and Canon Bonnyboat's chocolate ration, he found him behind the counter, dolloping out kolas to men in light blue suits and girls in pink blouses.

"You see, Reverendo Father, I cannot be in two places at once," Signor Sarno explained as he handed the priest twelve bars of Cadbury's ration chocolate. "Per Bacco, non sono facili le cose in questo tempo di guerra e di lotta."

Sir Dugald Ippecacuanha didn't seem to be finding things easy either in this time of war and struggle when the canon ran into him a few minutes later jamming his whole face against a chemist's window and popping an incontinent eye at a cake of Palm Olive soap.

"Things are in one hell of a mess," he told the canon. "All this talk about what we're going to do after the war is ridiculous. Let's win the war first and then let's talk about what we're going to do. And if you ask me, there's only one way to do that and that's to bomb the Jerries and Eyeties to Hell: men, women, and children."

The canon murmured back something evasive because he didn't know what to think about bombing any more than he was quite certain that Mr. Stalin was unconsciously defending the doctrine of the Immaculate Conception; but he knew that he disliked intensely the cheap jeers and sneers made at the enemy by the same popular press that had acclaimed Munich in 1938, and shouted, "Avoid Continental Entanglements" in 1936, and would certainly have preached collaboration with the same vehement illiteracy if Hitler had conquered Britain in 1940. Indeed, to supplement his argument, Sir Dugald showed him a copy of that day's issue of the *Daily Bugle*, which shouted in a headline: "We've Paid 'em Back Now," and in another, "There's Plenty of Chocs and Cigs in East Coast Towns."

People had to queue up for the tramcars these days. Canon Smith lined up behind a mother and two children. He tickled the children and made them laugh, and the mother didn't seem to mind, even though she must have known that he was a priest. That, thought the canon, was one of the advantages of growing old: people accepted you for what you had always been, so that even priests found it easier to be holier in public when they were old.

The tram, when it came, was crowded, but the conductress allowed Canon Smith to stand at the back and ring the bell for her: one ring to stop, two rings to go, and three rings to go whizzing past the next stop when they couldn't take any more passengers. She'd always been a great admirer of the Catholics, so she said, and had a girlfriend in Glasgow who always went to the Church of the Passionate Fathers, she thought they were called, and perhaps one day the canon would be kind enough to come down to the depot and give her tram a ding of holy water just to bring her luck.

The canon enjoyed ringing the bell, because it was such a change from his ordinary duties, but the conductress explained that he mustn't ring the bell for the tram to start at the stop outside the railway station because that was the pointsman's job, and there'd be the heck of a row if he wasn't allowed to blow his whistle. Indeed, it was as well this was so because the canon would have forgotten to ring the bell anyway, as when they reached the station there was a wagon drawn up at a siding and filled with sheep making noises just like Professor Joad laughing in the Brains Trust, and indeed when the tram moved off again, they seemed to be saying something about the Pursuit of the Absolute.

Nowadays, the canon divided his friends and acquaintances into two classes: the horizontal and the vertical. The horizontal were those whom he had known for only a short time, and the vertical were those whom he had known for a long time. Chief among the latter were Reverend Mother and Canon Bonnyboat, both of whom he called to see once a week, because they liked talking about the same things as he did, but he was sorrier for Canon Bonnyboat than he was for Reverend Mother, because poor Canon Bonnyboat could only limp about with a stick, whereas Reverend Mother was still as spry as a sparrow.

He found Canon Bonnyboat sitting huddled in the parlor of the home with a lot of other old priests who were too lame and hobbledy to say Mass anymore unless there were no steps in front of the altar. All the old priests sat looking at Canon Smith out of peery, envious eyes because he was still active enough to gad about giving out the sacraments, whereas they had to stay shut up together and listen to each other's stories and read the serial in the *Catholic Trumpet*.

"And how's the new bishop doing?" one of them asked.

"Excellently," Canon Smith said. "He's very popular. As a matter of fact, he's consecrating my church next month. The building's finished now."

"In my day, they didn't make boys bishops," another old priest said. "And bishops didn't try to make themselves popular. On the contrary, the more unpopular they were, the more they were sure they were doing God's Will."

"Bishops have gone down the drain like everything else," another old priest said.

"I remember when I was a young curate in County Cork, I met a darling bishop and he was only thirty-five and he had eyes as blue as God's sky and a great strong arm that could lift a pony and trap right off the ground, bedad so he could," the first old priest said.

"Brought the chocolate?" Canon Bonnyboat asked with a globby eye as soon as he and Canon Smith were alone in a corner together with the ludo board in front of them. Canon Smith knew that Canon Bonnyboat had been wanting to ask this question for the last ten minutes but hadn't liked to in case he would have to share his chocolate with the other priests. For since he had grown old, Canon Bonnyboat had also grown greedy, and a bar of Fry's cream chocolate meant more to him now than the book he was supposed to be writing on the Ceremonies of the Uniate Churches.

"I'll tell you what: we'll play for it," Canon Bonnyboat said, looking round to make sure that none of the other priests were listening. "How many bars is it this month? Six? Right, if I win, I get your bars as well as my own, that is twelve; and if you win, you get twelve."

"I'm not very fond of chocolate really, and you can have mine without playing for it," Canon Smith said.

"Nonsense, we'll play for it," Canon Bonnyboat said.

So play for it they did, and at first Canon Smith seemed to be winning, for he threw most of the sixes. Canon Bonnyboat's expression grew very mournful, indeed, and he only grunted when Canon Smith asked his advice about how to arrange the ceremonies when the bishop came to consecrate the Church of the Holy Name; but in the end, it was Canon Bonnyboat who threw all the sixes, and he even sent Canon Smith's four men right back to the beginning, so that he won the twelve bars of chocolate after all. Canon Smith was glad that Canon Bonnyboat had won, because he at once became more like his old self again and told Canon Smith how he had once on Christmas Day in Spain heard a cardinal sing the High Mass of the Aurora according to the Mozarabic rite.

XXXIV

WHEN, TWO DAYS before the new bishop was due to consecrate the Church of the Holy Name, Canon Smith heard what most of his parishioners called the sirens sound in the middle of the night, he was not alarmed, because he had so often heard them sound before and nothing had happened. His rheumatism was hurting him, though, and his legs felt all stiff and aching, so as he lay in the darkness waiting for the "all clear" to sound, he offered his suffering up to Almighty God, that He might be pleased to accept it in reparation for his own and the world's forgetfulness of Him. But the "all clear" didn't go; instead, there were bangs and explosions and more explosions, coming nearer and nearer.

Canon Smith was not a brave man; at least, he didn't think that he was, because he knew that he would very much rather die naturally in his bed than be hanged and disemboweled and burnt as a martyr, and he thought that being burned alive in an air-raid fire must be even worse, because the greater glory of God didn't come into it at all. He had, therefore, quite a hollow feeling in his stomach as, with the crashing and the cracking growing louder and louder, he bundled into his clothes and hurried away downstairs to the church, wondering if it would be a sin to extinguish an incendiary bomb with holy water and wishing that he could consult Canon Bonnyboat on the matter.

He had no curate these days, because young Father Burt had gone away as a chaplain with the Argyll and Sutherland Highlanders, and he hoped that if a fire were started, he would be able to put it out alone. As he opened the presbytery door, however, and walked out into the night, the banging suddenly ceased, and the stars in the sky were calm above his head.

When he reached the porch of the church, he found it packed with couples canoodling and stuffing themselves with fish and chips. He had to explain several times who he was before they would move aside to let him pass. He hesitated as to whether he should chase them away, but he remembered what Canon Dobbie had said thirteen years ago at his first chapter meeting, how that a grace from the Blessed Sacrament might touch their souls and change their dispositions to Almighty God, so he let them remain where they were.

Inside, the church was dark but for the sanctuary lamp, burning like a ruby. For a few minutes, the canon knelt and prayed that the day would soon come when the night would belong again to monks and nuns praising God down the centuries. Then he lit the two Low Mass candles on the high altar, because even though all the windows had been blacked out, he thought it safest to show as little light as possible. The waiting altar seemed to keep receding as he sat down in the front pew and looked at it, so he shut his eyes, and it was still there when he opened them again.

The gunfire sounded, breaking out in a great roar over the town, and there were other noises as well, whistlings and screamings, followed by explosions, although it did not seem that anybody could really be being bombed. The canon remembered having read in the *Highland Herald*, immediately below a reference to the evil of Sunday concerts for the troops, that those who were out in the streets during air raids might easily be wounded by a splinter from an anti-aircraft shell, so he went back to the church door and opened it. The lovers were no longer canoodling now but were staring in startled dismay at the sky at the edge of the town, which was now red and glowing. The canon invited them to come in, telling them that he thought that it was dangerous for them to remain outside. They came in sheepishly. They were mostly soldiers and sailors accompanied by trollops from the Port Said Dancing Club. Most of the trollops had no hats on, and so Canon Smith told them to put their handkerchiefs over their heads, as Saint Paul had ruled that it wasn't becoming for a woman to have her head uncovered in God's house. One of the sailors said that he remembered having read in the newspaper that the Archbishop of Canterbury had said that girls could now enter churches without hats on, but Canon Smith said that as far as he was concerned, it was what Saint Paul had said that mattered. So the trollops put their handkerchiefs over their heads, flat out like tea cloths, but the canon showed them how to make them stay on properly by tying four knots at the corners, and he lent his own handkerchief to a big, blowsy Jezebel from the docks who said that she hadn't got one, because she thought it was rude to blow her nose in night clubs.

At this one of the soldiers laughed aloud and then stuck his hand in front of his mouth and apologized to the canon, saying that he had forgotten that he was in church; but the canon said that there was no need to apologize at all, because God didn't mind how much people laughed in church, provided that they laughed at the right sort of joke. Whereupon the soldier said that he had always thought that the Catholic religion was a very fine religion, indeed, and one of the sailors said that he thought so, too, and that, indeed, he would have become a Catholic long ago only he hadn't been able to understand the bit about the unbaptized babies burning forever and ever in Hell when it really wasn't their fault at all that they hadn't been baptized.

The canon said that the sailor was quite wrong and that the souls of unbaptized babies didn't burn in Hell at all, and that if they would all sit down, he would tell them what the Church's teaching on the subject really was and perhaps it would help to take their minds off the air raid. So they all sat down in the two back pews, and the canon stood in the pew in front of them and told them all about the sacrament of Baptism. Two of the trollops looked rather bored, and one of them kept winking at one of the soldiers, but Canon Smith didn't notice because he was having to talk so loudly in order to make himself heard above the air raid.

The canon said that the sacrament of Baptism was instituted by our Lord Himself as an essential to salvation when He said that except people were baptized in the Name of the Father, and of the Son, and of the Holy Ghost, they should not inherit the Kingdom of Heaven. That might seem to us an unreasonable condition, but after all, our Lord spoke in the Name of Almighty God Himself, Who was best fitted to know what qualifications were necessary for admission to His own Paradise and to assess their justice. It was true, therefore, that the souls of unbaptized babies could not enter Heaven, because God Himself had said that they couldn't, but that did not mean that they went to Hell. Such a doctrine would, indeed, be most unreasonable, since the babies could not sin, as they lacked knowledge and therefore could not offend God with malice. The truth was that the souls of unbaptized babies went to another place called Limbo, where there was no suffering and where our Lord's Own Son had gone between the time of His dying on the Cross and His rising again from the dead. Limbo wasn't Heaven, of course, but equally so it wasn't Hell, and he was afraid that that was all he could say on the matter because it was all that Almighty God had revealed to the Church.

There was a big bang as the canon said this, and the sailor for whose benefit he had been explaining about Baptism opened his eyes. The trollop sitting next to him nudged him and asked him if he wasn't going to thank the Reverend Father for having told them all about Baptism so nicely. So the sailor stood up and said that now that he understood the souls of unbaptized babies didn't go to Hell but to Kimberley instead, he would think very seriously about becoming a Catholic. He was sure that all the rest of them would think very seriously about becoming Catholics, too, now that they knew the souls of unbaptized babies went to Kimberley.

Canon Smith hadn't time to correct the sailor and tell him that it was to Limbo and not to Kimberley that the souls of unbaptized babies went, because there was a bigger bang than ever, and the whole church trembled, and he and the soldiers and the sailors and the trollops all flung themselves flat. When they got up again, they were so frightened that they had forgotten all about the souls of unbaptized babies. The big, blowsy Jezebel from the docks asked the canon if they hadn't better sing a hymn and suggested "Abide With Me," but the canon said that he thought that "Praise to the Holiest in the Height" would be better, as it had been written by a very saintly man called John Henry Cardinal Newman.

They were all singing away at the tops of their voices when the incendiary bomb fell through the roof of the church and set the curtains behind the high altar on fire. Another bomb fell on the front pews and set them on fire, too, but Canon Smith didn't know about the incendiary bomb on the vestment chest until he rushed into the sacristy to put on a stole to remove the Blessed

Sacrament from the high altar. He found a stole hanging on the back of the door, and he found the key of the tabernacle, but the door of the tabernacle was so hot when he reached it that he could scarcely touch it. The sailors and the soldiers and the trollops tried to pull him back, but he shook them off and told them to get out of the church if they didn't want to be burned to death. They said, however, that they weren't going to leave the church until he did, because he had been so nice telling them about how the souls of unbaptized babies went to Kimberley. The canon's face was so sore with the flames that he couldn't answer them, but he managed to get the pyx and the ciborium out of the tabernacle.

They were all very excited when they stood outside watching the blaze, but the canon said that they mustn't talk to him, because he was carrying Almighty God in his hands.

The whole town seemed in flames when a fire engine came at last, and Canon Smith set out to carry the Blessed Sacrament to the convent. The big, blowsy Jezebel from the docks went with him, because she said that she would like to chum him. The canon said that he would be quite pleased to have her company, only he said again that she mustn't talk, and he tried to explain to her what a very holy thing it was that they were doing and how ordinarily lighted candles were carried in front of the Blessed Sacrament to do God honor, but that there were times when even God had to be robbed of His ceremonial. The big, blowsy Jezebel from the docks said that perhaps the buildings burning all around them would do instead, but the canon said that he didn't think that God would see it quite that way, as the burning buildings were the beacons of men's miseries, and God was not honored by their distress.

The air raid was still on when they reached the convent, and Reverend Mother and the nuns were all up and in their habits. They brought lighted candles and formed into procession when they saw that Canon Smith was carrying the Blessed Sacrament and, as she followed them into the chapel, the blowsy Jezebel thought that she had never seen anything so pretty in all her life. As the canon put the pyx and the ciborium away in the tabernacle, the nuns knelt and sang the "Laudate Dominum." When the canon came round from his faint, it was a new, young nun whose face he didn't know who was bending over him.

XXXV

CANON SMITH LIKED the flighted lamps the nuns carried when Canon Muldoon brought him Holy Communion in bed. He liked to think of the pools of amber they made on the polished floors of the corridors, because it was just the sort of reflection the Blessed Sacrament cast on men's souls as it was hoisted above the unhappiness of the world. He liked to think of the nuns' habits as they swept along through the convent and of bent, old Canon Muldoon following behind with the humeral veil wrapped round his precious Burden, because it was the whisper of God's poetry trickling on.

He liked it, too, when he was anointed, with the sky outside the window and the trees still there. As Canon Muldoon traced the last mercies on his weary body, far away out along the bend of the railway line, at the junction of the golf course and Sir Dugald Ippecacuanha's estate, a puff of smoke appeared, and a miniature worm of train rolled tinily along the embankment. Canon Smith liked looking at it, because that seemed to be part of God's poetry too. He lay thinking of the rhythm of the seasons and how right Canon Bonnyboat had been when he had compared the liturgy of the Church to the flowers and the leaves, which God painted new every year.

"Buon giorno, reverendo padre mio, e come sta?" Elvira said as she came in in her junior subaltern's uniform and knelt beside the bed, but he knew from the way that she smiled at him that she didn't expect him to answer, and besides, Canon Muldoon was praying out the great, grim words on which his soul must shortly sail: "In the name of angels and archangels; in the name of thrones and dominions; in the name of principalities and powers; in the name of virtues, cherubim and seraphim; in the name of patriarchs and prophets ..." Reverend Mother was kneeling beside the bed, too, with her face all wrinkled and wise, and she took his hand in both of hers and pressed it, and he knew that she was saying goodbye to him in Christ Jesus their Lord. The new, young nuns were there as well, with lovely, red, shiny faces like apples, and eyes that would never grow old, because they were Christ's brides. Lady Ippecacuanha was there, too, making great, gobbling noises in her throat, and the Polish chaplain and the new bishop and old, dried-up Councilor Thompson, who had used to say such dreadful things about God's Church.

"In the name of holy monks and hermits ..." He would be seeing quite a lot of old friends soon, if God was merciful and he landed on the right side of the fence. Angus McNab and the bishop and the boozy major and the old sailor and Monsignor O'Duffy and Mother de la Tour and Mother Leclerc and Annie Rooney and a host of others who had been studded in the calendar of his prayers. He wondered if there would be flowers in Heaven for Mother de la Tour, and whether Angus would be allowed to wear the ribbon of the D.C.M., and if Annie Rooney liked singing the "Magnificat" now that God had made all things plain to her. For that was what death really was: a making of things plain, a shining forth from behind bomber airplanes and advertisements for syrup of figs.

And suddenly, as he lay there, he knew the answer to it all: how the lame and the sick should be healed and how the poor should be rewarded and how God's saints might eat peas off their knives; how the banker might be last and the harlot first; how a priest's hands never failed however flat his words; how the Church was all glorious within because the freight she carried healed all her cracks; why God often chose ugly, blunt men to do the task of angels; why God was patient and why priests must be patient too; how mighty was their calling and how certain their ointment; and how it was in the answer that each man gave to Christ in the silence of his soul that the fairness of tomorrow's meadows lay. It was all so simple, really, and he wanted to tell them before he went, but already the shore of those lined along his bed was retreating, and he had time only to cry out at the Polish chaplain.

"Don't forget to let them know there'll be Mass on Sunday in the fish market," he said.

The End

Questions for Group Discussion or Individual Reflection

NOTE: THESE QUESTIONS contain key information about the plot and characters; do not read these questions until after you have finished the book!

1. Father Smith continues to think about the death of the sailor in chapter 1 for the rest of the book. Why do you think this was so important to him? What stood out to you as you read this scene?

2. Early in the book, Father Smith encounters a great deal of antagonism regarding his Catholic Faith. How does the world around him change in this regard? Do you think this change is due to a better tolerance and understanding of the Faith or due to growing apathy and indifference toward religion in the greater culture? Explain by citing examples from the book.

3. How do Father/Canon Smith's views on war develop during his lifetime? What were his views before the first World War, during the war, immediately after the war, and then

immediately before the outbreak of World War II? Who and what has affected his changing viewpoints on war and his consideration of evil? How so?

4. In chapter 15, Father Smith says, "It is not countries that we want to be great but individual men.... Great as our Lord would have them be great, not with trumpets and banners and guns and battleships, but in generosity, selflessness, and humility." How does this theme of "greatness" play into the lives of the various characters in the novel? Think of the priests and nuns, the wealthy Lord and Lady Ippecacuanha, Angus McNab (who received a war medal), Signor Sarno, Joseph Scott, Elvira Sarno, and others. How does each strive to be "great" in his or her own way? Who do you think actually achieves greatness?

5. Miss Agdala, the author whom Father Smith meets on the steps of the High Kirk in chapter 16, asks Father Smith in reply to his attempts to explain the Catholic Faith, "But who on earth wants to be a saint these days?" How would you answer her question? Which characters in the book do you think live like saints (or at least try to)? Who seems to have given up, and why do you think they have?

6. Consider the character of Lady Ippecacuanha, who is a wealthy woman and a convert to the Faith, in light of Christ's words in Matthew 19:24: "It is easier for a camel to pass through the eye of a needle than for one who is rich to enter the kingdom of God." Father Smith also spends a good amount of thought in the book reflecting on wealth and poverty, such as in chapter 18: "A rage against the rich rose in the

priest as he thought of how easy things had been for them and how difficult for Angus. It was so simple for them, with their green lawns and their limousines and their conservatories and their holidays at Dinard, to talk about what they would do if they were workingmen, but it wasn't so easy for the working-man, especially when he hadn't any work to do." What is Lady Ippecacuanha's role in the book? Does her conversion and her faith change her or her family, and if so, how? In the end, do you believe she is a virtuous character? Why or why not?

7. Think of the character of Angus McNab. We first meet him serving Mass in chapter 1. Then we encounter him at various points in the book: a soldier at war, working at the cinema, announcing his engagement, unemployed and bitter, a mur-derer in prison. What do you think about his life story as seen through the eyes of Father Smith? Is he a victim of the world, a martyr, a lost soul, a redeemed man, or something else? Bruce Marshall also chooses not to write whether or not Angus says an act of contrition or "Into Thy hands I com-mend my spirit" before his death; what do you think Angus does? Why does Marshall leave this out?

8. How are the various religious men and women in the book called to their vocations? How do major characters such as Father Smith, Reverend Mother, Monsignor O'Duffy, Father Bonnyboat, Father Scott, and the bishop each live out his or her vocation? How does each work to promote the love of Christ in his or her own way?

9. How do Father Smith's relationships with Father Bonnyboat, Monsignor O'Duffy, Reverend Mother, and the bishop grow

and develop over the course of the book? How do these relationships change Father Smith and help him in his quest for holiness?

10. Do you think Elvira Sarno lives an authentic Catholic life, and if so, how? How does her story force Father Smith to re-think some of his ideas on wealth and contemporary society? How do you see her grow in her faith over the course of the book?

11. How does the nuns', especially Reverend Mother's, attitude and relationship with France develop over the course of the book? What do the different flags flown over the convent represent? Rebellion, hope, patriotism, forgiveness?

12. In chapter 20, Canon Smith gives his colleagues a long speech on morality during his first chapter house meeting. Review his speech, found on pages 161–164 . Do you agree or disagree with what Canon Smith says? Do you think the other canons and Monsignor O'Duffy are silent because they don't understand, because they don't agree, or because they are unsure about his sentiments? Explain based on what you know about these characters.

13. This book was first published in 1945, before the Second Vatican Council but more than fifty years after Leo XIII's papal encyclical on capital and labor, *Rerum Novarum*, which discusses the rights and duties of workers and employers, defends the right to form unions, rejects socialism and communism as well as unrestricted capitalism, and promotes the concept of just wages. How does the theme of workers' rights, especially a Catholic understanding of workers' rights, play

into the book, and how does it contrast with the mainstream, secular views found in the book?

14. The bishop introduces some complex theological points in the book. Of all his conversations with Father/Canon Smith, which stood out to you? Did anything he say cause you to pause and think of your own faith?

15. Chapter 24, by far the shortest chapter in the book, tells of Canon Smith and his confreres in the papal hall of audiences. Why do you think Bruce Marshall chose to include this short encounter, which may seem at first jarring, random, and unconnected to the surrounding text? How does it connect to the rest of the story?

16. Re-read Father Scott's sermon in chapter 26 (pages 193–196). Recall that this book was originally published in 1945. How have things gone since? How is our culture even more focused on progress for progress's sake, especially in terms of technological progress? Consider his advice: "For true progress was moral rather than mechanical: if there were to be more switches, more buttons, more batteries, there must also be more restraints, more austerities, more unselfishness, more humilities, more prayers, more contemplations on the real end of man." What can we, as individual Catholics, do to respond to the cult of progress in our own time?

17. How does this book exemplify the joys of the Catholic priesthood? How does it depict the hardships faced by parish priests? Think of the major characters in the book: the bishop, Monsignor O'Duffy, Father Bonnyboat, Father Smith, and

Father Scott. What does each lose over the course of the book? What does each gain?

18. The bishop is not named until chapter 31, when he is laying on his deathbed. Why did Bruce Marshall not include his name until now? What deeper meaning might this exclusion have? Notice his name: James Michael Gabriel. How is this a fitting name for his character? How does the bishop live out the example of each of his namesakes at different times in the book?

19. As Canon Smith lies dying, he thinks of all the friends he hopes to meet in Heaven, specifically "Angus McNab and the bishop and the boozy major and the old sailor and Monsignor O'Duffy and Mother de la Tour and Mother Leclerc and Annie Rooney." What do you think of this list of sinners and saints? What does this list tell you of Smith's faith?

20. What do you think, in the end, of Father/Canon Smith? What are his virtues, and what are his vices? What do you think of his actions on the night of the bombing? What do you think of his deathbed experiences? Do you like him as a character? Why or why not?

Glossary of Terms:

Argy-bargying: arguing about nonsense

A.T.S.: Auxiliary Territorial Service, the women's branch of the British Army during World War II

Auld: old

Aye: yes

Bairn: baby

Beanfeast: celebratory meal or party

Besom: broom; sometimes a term for a mischievous woman

Blether: lengthy chit-chat, often inconsequential; one who takes part in an inconsequential conversation

Bonny: beautiful, pretty; handsome

Braw: pleasant, fine, splendid

Byrrh and Quinquina: French apertif wines

Clarty: dirty, muddy

Claver: to gossip

Cowp: to tip over

Dae: do

Dago: a racial slur for an Italian man.

Dinna: don't

Doups: bottom, rear end

Dreich: dull, gloomy

Gowk: fool

Haver: to talk foolishly, chatter

House of Rimmon: reference to 2 Kings 5:17–18. "To bow at the house of Rimmon" means to put aside one's own beliefs or preferences for the sake of conforming to the norm.

Keek: peep, look

Ken: know

Lass/laddie: young woman/young man

Licorice allsort: an assortment of licorice candies. "Licorice allsort shirt" means a multi-colored shirt.

Ludo (game): Parcheesi

Mashie: an old style of golf club

Muckle: large, much

Odol: a brand of mouthwash

OTC: Officers' Training Corps, a military leadership training unit

Plaister (plaster): bandage

Stravaige, stravaiging: wander, wandering

Vitagraph: reference to Vitagraph Studios, a major film producer in the early twentieth century

W.V.S.: the Women's Voluntary Service, a group dedicated to serving the needs of Britain. Later known as the Royal Voluntary Service.

Ye: you

Yon: this, that, over there

About the Author

LIEUTENANT-COLONEL CLAUDE CUNNINGHAM, known as Bruce Marshall (1899–1987), was a prolific Scottish writer of fiction and nonfiction books on a wide range of topics and in various genres. His first book, *A Thief in the Night*, came out in 1918. His last, *An Account of Capers*, was published posthumously in 1988. In addition to this novel, his best known works are *Father Malachy's Miracle* (1931) and *Vespers for Vienna* (1947).

Sophia Institute

SOPHIA INSTITUTE IS a nonprofit institution that seeks to nurture the spiritual, moral, and cultural life of souls and to spread the gospel of Christ in conformity with the authentic teachings of the Roman Catholic Church.

Sophia Institute Press fulfills this mission by offering translations, reprints, and new publications that afford readers a rich source of the enduring wisdom of mankind.

Sophia Institute also operates the popular online resource CatholicExchange.com. *Catholic Exchange* provides world news from a Catholic perspective as well as daily devotionals and articles that will help readers to grow in holiness and live a life consistent with the teachings of the Church.

In 2013, Sophia Institute launched Sophia Institute for Teachers to renew and rebuild Catholic culture through service to Catholic education. With the goal of nurturing the spiritual, moral, and cultural life of souls, and an abiding respect for the role and work of teachers, we strive to provide materials and programs that are at once enlightening to the mind and ennobling to the heart; faithful and complete, as well as useful and practical.

Sophia Institute gratefully recognizes the Solidarity Association for preserving and encouraging the growth of our apostolate over the course of many years. Without their generous and timely support, this book would not be in your hands.

www.SophiaInstitute.com
www.CatholicExchange.com
www.SophiaInstituteforTeachers.org

Sophia Institute Press is a registered trademark of Sophia Institute.
Sophia Institute is a tax-exempt institution as defined by the
Internal Revenue Code, Section 501(c)(3). Tax ID 22-2548708.